i've
NEVER
BEEN
(UN)HAPPIER

SHAHEEN BHATT

i've NEVER BEEN (UN)HAPPIER

foreword by Mahesh Bhatt

EBURY
PRESS

An imprint of Penguin Random House

EBURY PRESS

USA | Canada | UK | Ireland | Australia
New Zealand | India | South Africa | China

Ebury Press is part of the Penguin Random House group of companies
whose addresses can be found at global.penguinrandomhouse.com

Published by Penguin Random House India Pvt. Ltd
7th Floor, Infinity Tower C, DLF Cyber City,
Gurgaon 122 002, Haryana, India

Penguin
Random House
India

First published in Ebury Press by Penguin Random House India 2019

10 9 8 7 6 5 4 3

ISBN 9780143449126

Typeset in Adobe Caslon Pro by Manipal Technologies Limited, Manipal
Printed at Thomson Press India Ltd, New Delhi

www.penguin.co.in

MIX
Paper
FSC FSC® C010615

Contents

Contents

For Soni and Mahesh, and Alia, who learned to love me in darkness when I was all out of light.
For Neha and Namita, the unwitting caretakers of a surly, reclusive teenager.
For sixteen-year-old me, who did not yet know that this suffering can be a gift.
And for anyone who has ever felt different.

'Though my soul may set in darkness, it will rise in perfect light; I have loved the stars too fondly to be fearful of the night'

—Sarah Williams, 'The Old Astronomer'

23.01.2018

ALWAYS ILL AT EASE.
ALWAYS A WAYS AWAY FROM HAPPY.
ALWAYS FAR FROM WHO I WANT TO BE.
30 YEARS OLD AND I STILL FEEL 18.
I'M TIRED OF MYSELF IN SO MANY WAYS.
TIRED OF THE MELODRAMA.
TIRED OF EVEN BEING TIRED.
EVEN I'VE REACHED THE POINT AT WHICH I
LOOK AT MYSELF AND THINK "OH, GROW UP".
LIFE ISN'T REALLY SO BAD AND NOTHING
WARRANTS THIS PITEOUS INTERNAL AND
EXTERNAL MOANING. WHAT IS IT BUT
SELF-INVOLVED WHINING PAST A POINT.
BOOHOO LIFE HURTS AND IT'S UNFAIR.
WELL FUCK, WE ALL KNOW THAT. WHAT
NEXT?
I WANT TO TAKE MY MIND OUT BACK
AND SHOOT IT.
ENOUGH. JUST. FUCKING. ENOUGH.
I'M FILLED WITH DISGUST TODAY. AND
MAYBE THAT'S THE PROBLEM.
WHERE DO YOU GO WHEN YOU HATE
YOUR OWN COMPANY?
HOW DO YOU ESCAPE YOU?

02.03.2019

I'M COMING UNDONE.
SLOWLY, BUT SURELY, I'M COMING UNDONE.
FROM THE INSIDE OUT.
IT'S EATING AWAY AT ALL THAT I AM.
ITS TURNING MY INSIDES TO MUSH.
ITS OBSCURING Foreword G.
I DON'T FIT. A
I'M UNSTUCK. UNTETHERED. ADRIFT.
EVERYTHING HURTS. EVERYTHING STILL HURTS.
IT WAS SUPPOSED TO BE BETTER BY NOW.
WHY DOES ROCK BOTTOM GO FURTHER
DOWN EACH TIME. WHY DOES THE WORST
ALWAYS GET WORSE.
HOW AM I HERE, NO BETTER OFF THAN
I WAS AT 13.
I'M STUPID. I'M WORTHLESS. I'M LAUGHABLE.
I'M EMPTY. I'M USELESS. I'M A BURDEN.
I'M A WASTE OF SPACE. I'M UNLOVABLE.
I'M SELFISH. I'M AWFUL. I SHOULD NOT EXIST -
JUST SOME THOUGHTS.
THIS IS WHERE THEY'LL SAY IT STARTED.
'BUT SHE SEEMED FINE' THEY'LL SAY.
I DON'T KNOW WHY I'M HERE ANYMORE.
I DON'T SEE THE MESSAGE.
WHAT AM I MISSING.
THIS MAKES LESS SENSE EVERYDAY.
EVERY MOMENT.

There is an end and there is an ending to that end, and I was face-to-face with that end. My friend, philosopher, guide, U.G. Krishnamoorthy, who was the lodestar that had seen me through many a dark night, had opted to die without seeking any kind of medical intervention. At his behest, albeit unwillingly, I had left him in Italy, in the quaint town of Vallecrosia, in the company of an American friend, and made my way back home, without any idea whether I would ever see him alive again.

It was the darkest hour of my life, but for some strange reason, my friend, in his hours of death, had left me with a heightened taste for life.

'Your life is finished, Daddy,' said my twenty-year-old daughter, Shaheen, as she gazed at me, thoughtfully with those grown-up eyes of hers. I had just arrived back home, and it was well past midnight.

'People want to live for a long time, just so that they may experience even a fraction of what you are living through right now. You have already reached the summit. Where will you go from here? This is what mystics have spoken about at length when they journey through the dark night of the soul,' she said, as I read out to her from those scraps of paper on which I had scribbled my heightened emotions.

Having unburdened myself of what I had lived through to my little girl gave me a few moments of respite, but it also made me feel worried for her. She had listened to me with every pore of her young being. That's when I got the feeling that there was a kind of desolate vastness within her that was able to contain the depths of such emotion. And I was reminded of what Nietzsche had said . . . that he was more afraid of being understood than misunderstood. Because if he was misunderstood, only his intellectual vanity would be hurt. But if he was understood, he would feel even worse, because that meant that the person who understood him would have had to have suffered enough in order to have understood what he was saying in the first place.

And as dawn broke, I sensed for the first time that my little girl had suffered intensely. But I only knew how much when I read her book all those years later.

When a grain of sand gets into the craw of an oyster it causes it great pain. So, in order to escape from that pain, the oyster covers the grain of sand with a substance that turns the grain into a pearl. Nowhere does the oyster intend to create a precious jewel.

This is what struck me when I read the rough manuscript of Shaheen's book which she had mailed me. Shaheen, in order to escape from the darkness which she had perhaps genetically inherited from me, had dared to embrace that darkness like I had done to stay functionally sane. I realized as I sat there riveted while reading it, that, for her, writing this book was an act towards sheer survival.

When a sandalwood tree burns in a forest fire, it releases a perfume that turns the whole fire into a fragrant blaze. The pain that Shaheen used as fuel to write her book has released her fragrant core. Not only to me as a parent, but to thousands of people out there who are shadowed by this biochemical 'disorder' called depression.

When I was an insomniac teenager I would often slip out in the middle of the night and go to a dargah or to buy a cigarette, and somehow get through the long night. One night I encountered a Sufi fakir, who said something to me which will shadow me till I die. He said . . . if you seek blessings from the lord above then ask him to shower you with pain. Because pain wakes you up . . . *Ya Allah takleef de . . . dard jagaata hai . . .*

I asked him, what kind of an absurd prayer is this? Who on earth would ask God for pain? He peered into my eyes and said smilingly, 'It is pain that keeps you awake my boy . . . otherwise you would be sleeping soundly in that high-rise building in some air-conditioned room . . . and where the hell would that get you?'

Where would we be without our pain, Shaheen?

Human suffering, after all, is the wound from where great religious movements, political movements and artistic movements have bloomed. My pain is the bedrock on which I have built the edifice of Mahesh Bhatt the filmmaker. Your pain has helped you produce this remarkable book, which will be a coping device for those millions out there who suffer in silence.

My child, you are the firefly that illuminates the darkness in the jungle by burning its own fuel, and as it does so, it lights up the way for the lost traveller.

9 March 2019   Mahesh Bhatt
Mumbai

Time: 9:35 pm Date: 6.02.2001

Dear Diary, [why do i even start off this way]

I have a splitting headache, i could almost die from the pain. Today was a bad day. I woke up late and i hardly studied but i ~~went to~~ market in the morning since i had to buy pe~~ncil~~ exam. I didn't have much lunch. I spoke to namita in the afternoon. only spoke for about 15 minutes. i got sad after hanging up [yep, AGAIN] I've got a lot on my mind these days. I feel isolated and separated from the world. No one sees me. I'm constantly at war with myself. I know it's very cliche but that's the thing. I only feel like crying these days. I get sad very suddenly. I feel like i'm no good. I know i'm fat and don't look good + school worries me. I'm no good at maths or Hindi, i'm afraid i'm going to fail this year and then everyone will think i'm a loser. I think mama and papa also expect a lot from me. They keep telling me how bright i am and how i will do well. what if i don't live up to their expectations. I think of Ania and how good she is at everything she tries, she can make them proud i can't. i'm not good enough. i'm not good at anything i'm a loser and i don't like it. i wish life wasn't so hard.

Preface

At thirty-one, I've lived with depression for all of my adult life. In fact, I've lived with depression for longer than I haven't.

Somehow, against all odds, I'm in constant anguish. Now, I'm not talking about the 'Netflix-cancelled-my-favourite-show-and-I-keep-dropping-chicken-curry-on-my-favourite-pair-of-jeans-so-my-life-sucks' sort of anguish. I'm talking about the 'there's-a-deep-unexplained-sadness-in-me-that's-eating-away-at-my-hopes-and-dreams-and-skin-quality-and-making-me-want-to-literally-jump-out-of-this-window' sort of anguish.

Situationally speaking, I've never been subjected to or lived through anything truly horrific; nothing that is unique to just me, at any rate. The lifestyle I enjoy is not one I worked my way up to through hard labour, and a lot, (if not most) of the opportunity afforded to me comes from groundwork that was painstakingly laid by my parents. Along with the financial security my circumstances afford me, they also grant me the means to make demands for and exercise my rights to freedom and equality, which a lot of people in India, and the world over, can't do. In short, I possess all the qualifications of what they call a 'lucky' one. So I'm aware I am free in ways a lot of people aren't.

Nevertheless, I was diagnosed with clinical depression when I was eighteen years old, after already having lived with it for many years. It took me a long time to understand the nature of the illness I was living with since as a condition, depression is particularly stigmatized in Indian society, not to mention widely misunderstood in general. So, before I lay bare my own experience, I think it is of vital importance to clear up these misconceptions and understand what depression really is. Let's start there.

Depression is a common mood disorder and a serious medical illness.

There are many types of depression and they vary in source. All depressive disorders, no matter their type or cause, will negatively affect how you feel, think and act. According to the *Diagnostic and Statistical Manual of Mental Disorders* published by the American Psychiatric Association, depression is largely split up into two categories: major depressive disorder (which is what I live with) and persistent depressive disorder, or dysthymia. Both forms of disorders cause sadness, low moods and a feeling of hopelessness but the difference between them lies in the severity and duration of the depressive episodes. A person with major depressive disorder will have a sad or depressed mood that lasts anywhere from two weeks to a number of months. Once the episode passes and the patient goes into remission they feel 'back to normal' again. Persistent depressive disorder, on the other hand, is a chronically depressed mood that lasts for at least two years or longer. The symptoms of persistent depressive disorder are less severe than those of major depression and those who have it suffer from a constant 'low level' sadness. When one has persistent depressive disorder coupled with periodic bouts of major depressive disorder, it's known as 'double depression'.

Depression is a complex disease, and while its exact causes are under scrutiny, it is speculated to occur for many reasons. In some cases depression can occur because of biological factors such as genetic predispositions, hormonal changes (including menopause, childbirth or thyroid problems) and differences in biochemistry (an imbalance of naturally occurring substances called neurotransmitters in the brain and spinal cord). In other cases depression is caused by psychological factors, severe life stressors, substance abuse and certain medical conditions that affect the way your brain regulates your moods.

To add to the considerations of complexity, the symptoms, intensity and experience of depression vary from person to person such that it manifests differently in different people. Unlike other chronic illnesses such as diabetes or autoimmune disorders, depression is not consistent with its symptoms. Some people sleep too little, some sleep too much, some lose their appetite, others binge eat, some manage to function in their day-to-day lives while others are completely consumed and debilitated by it. Depression is not a one-size-fits-all illness, and the diversity of its markers makes it that much harder to identify.

There are a lot of challenges that arise when trying to explain what depression is to someone who doesn't understand the condition or approaches it from a place of denial. One such challenge lies in the belief that mental illnesses can be tackled and overcome by sheer force of will alone. The absence of physical symptoms traditionally associated with disease makes it difficult for some to appreciate the seriousness of the condition. Depression doesn't cause a 103-degree fever or a visible rash; the symptoms are psychological and therefore harder to conceive of as medical in nature. For many who live with it, the greatest obstacles on the road to recovery are family and friends who do not 'believe' in depression. The assumption is that if you have a happy and comfortable life you have no cause for, or right to, the despair you're feeling. In short, you can't be depressed if there's nothing wrong or if you have no real problems. (Ironically, people who believe this also believe that those with 'real problems' don't have the time or luxury to suffer from depression.) So those who are unfamiliar with depression are misled by the lack of bodily symptoms and tend towards familiar statements like: 'Think positively.'/'You have to *want* to get better.'/'You're only doing this for the attention.'/'You're just being lazy.'/'You aren't even trying to pull yourself out of it.' Statements like these suggest your salvation lies in a choice you are simply electing not to make, but of course, that is categorically untrue.

We're taught early in life to keep our emotions hidden and we're especially taught that negative emotions have no place in the public domain. The overwhelming narrative is that succumbing to pain or sadness indicates weakness and that they're feelings you ought to keep to yourself. Such misconceptions are dangerous, with lasting consequences. My belief that they contribute to worsening the symptoms of depression and prevent people from getting the help they need is the reason I chose to write this account of my experience. The reactions I received when I told people I was writing a book about depression only confirmed what I felt—a handful were enthusiastic but most were instantly uncomfortable, many of them seeing it as unnecessary oversharing. But, 'oversharing' is now the most important thing that we can do. Depression is the monster that's hiding under your bed, and here's the thing, monsters can only live in the dark. It's when you turn on the light that you see that what you *thought* is a monster, isn't a monster at all, but something you can tame if you learn how. Monsters like depression live in the dark, and the way to turn on the light, is by talking about it.

I'm well aware that it is my privilege that allows me this platform through which I can talk about depression and the havoc it wreaks. Part of why I have been given this opportunity has to do with who my family is and the fact that I live with depression is particularly interesting when it's put into the context of my family.

I don't write about my experiences with depression to defend the legitimacy of my pain. My pain is real; it does not come to me because of my lifestyle, and it is not taken away by my lifestyle. But make no mistake, my lifestyle is an advantage when it comes to living with my condition. It provides me with easy access to the medical and social resources I need to support and fuel my recovery, which are both necessities and luxuries so many don't have access to. I can wake up on a bad day and afford to stay in bed. I can pay the price that good medical care and therapy come at and I am lucky to have family and friends who are well-informed and supportive. Most importantly, I've been able to cultivate an awareness of my condition in myself, and it's the only way I've been able to rid myself of the shame those with mental illnesses are often plagued with.

Imagine, despite all these advantages I still wake up some mornings wondering if I'm going to make it through the day. My life is a best-case scenario for someone living with depression. Take a second to imagine what the worst-case scenario looks like.

I am not an expert. I don't have a degree in medicine or psychiatry, neither have I spent years studying the ins and outs of mental illness. I don't have the weight or experience of age to back me up. I'm young and I still (hopefully) have a lot of life ahead of me.

What I do have is what I've come to learn on my almost twenty-year-long journey with depression. I can't claim to be an authority on anyone else's mind, only my own, but by sharing my reflections, I hope to add to the awareness of what depression is and what it can look like on the inside as well as the outside. I hope this effort will make it easier to identify and support depression rather than judge the circumstances and legitimacy of it. By writing about my experiences I hope to prove—and this is the important bit—that depression is nothing to be judged on or be ashamed of.

MORTALITY. THE SLIMY BITCH IS B
SHEBA HAS BEEN SICK A WHILE. S
STOP THE WORLD, I WANT OFF E
IT'S STRANGE, BUT I FEEL LIKE I
WITH THIS FEELING. THE FEELING
THATS JUST ABOUT TO GO OFF
I DON'T KNOW WHETHER I'M COM
IS THIS IT UNTIL I DIE? BE AFRA
I HAVE NO POETRY LEFT IN ME
NO PROFOUND WAY OF SAYING
IMPRESS MYSELF WHEN I READ
I SEE SO MUCH PAIN INCHING
THE FUTILITY OF IT ALL KEEPS
CAN YOU GET USED TO LOSS?
MUCH ANYMORE? WHAT DOES
WHAT DOES IT MAKE ME ... T
DOWN LIKE THIS?
I LOVE MY BABY. I DON'T WANT

. TO LOOK ME IN THE EYE.

MAY BE GETTING SICKER.

LIVED MOST OF MY ADULT LIFE

IMPENDING loss. LIKE A FIRE -

I DON'T K The Feeling ⅃.

OR GOING.

F LOSING EVERYONE UNTIL I DO?

ESE THINGS. NO WAY TO

ACK.

OWARDS ME.

LAMMING INTO ME.

THAT YOU DON'T FEEL IT AS

HAT MAKE YOU?

FACT THAT IT BREAKS ME

ER TO DIE.

The Feeling is a shapeshifter.

Some days it comes to me silently, taking me by surprise—cold, unfeeling and blank; an infinite void disguised as a wisp of smoke melting into the very air I breathe. It inhabits me, hijacking my entire being until there is none of me left, just more of it.

Other days it's a colossal monster that shakes the ground beneath me making me shiver with its every deafening step in my direction. It settles itself on my heart, crushing the life out of me yet never killing me, leaving me immobile, useless and broken.

On the worst days it comes to me as myself, as everything I could have been and as everything I will never be: immaculate, and completely without fault. It taunts and belittles me, obscuring my successes and highlighting my failures, reducing all that I am to a loathsome, insignificant speck.

The Feeling first came to me when I was twelve years old and didn't know its many faces.

At first, it came little by little. It lurked in the shadows, hiding just out of sight so that I would not see it. It came as a cold breeze, a heavy lump, a snide voice, inconveniencing me but not yet paralysing me.

And then, without warning, it came all at once.

In the blink of an eye the cold breeze became a blizzard that threatened to engulf me, the lump now a boulder that stifled my every sound, and its voice grew so loud that I could no longer hear anything else. It guilefully altered the very essence of my being as I slept, leaving me to contend with a complete stranger at the start of each new day. The moment I familiarized myself with it, it changed. I was a quick learner, I thought. But the Feeling was quicker.

I call the ages between fifteen and twenty-three the Dark Days because the Feeling never left me during that time. I went to bed with it and I woke up with it. It lived inside me. It became me.

It wasn't until I was eighteen that I found out that the Feeling had a name.

Depression, they called it, and then everything changed.

The room is in disarray.

Clothes, books and objects at random lay strewn in messy heaps all over the floor, the bed is unmade, the curtains are tightly drawn, and my bedside table is littered with half-empty strips of medication. The only light comes from a small yellow lamp in the corner of the room. It seems like it's around 4 p.m., though there's no real way to be sure. Day and night have become one; there's been no indication that the sun has risen and no indication that it has set. In this room, time has stopped.

From somewhere on the bed comes the muffled sound of a vibrating phone. It's flooded with messages that have gone unseen and calls that have gone unanswered. All this activity has earned it its special place, buried deep under the pillows.

At the heart of this disarray is me. My hair is unkempt, my lips are chapped, and I'm huddled up on the floor of my shower cabinet crying hysterically.

The shower cabinet is a strange place to take refuge, I know, but it's something I've done since I was a teenager. Maybe it's a leftover reflex from when I shared a bedroom with my sister and the bathroom was the only place I found any privacy. Maybe—in direct contradiction to my claustrophobia—small spaces make me feel safe when I'm upset. Whatever the reason, I'm here, and it's the longest I've spent out of bed in three days.

My breath comes in gasps as I rock back and forth, heaving with sobs. The tightness in my chest does nothing to deter the deep, guttural sounds that escape from me against my will. It's as if my senses are seamlessly swaying between being heightened and dulled: my puffy, leaden eyes are blinded by the bathroom lights, my vision is hazy, I'm awash in noise that jangles my nerves but it all seems to be coming from far, far away. Even the tiled floor feels stony and jagged against my unnaturally sensitive skin. In this moment of physical discomfort my insides match my outsides. My body may be at war with my surroundings but it's oddly welcome, distracting me from the other invisible war being waged in my mind.

I clutch my knees and cry until the tears no longer come, until my body is as spent as my mind, then I slowly peel myself off the floor and return to the bowels of my bed. On some days this bed is my home, on other days it is more like my captor. I'm unable to tear myself away from it, unable to even sit upright. Each time I muster the will and energy to lift myself up, I'm pulled back into its depths by some overpowering magnetic force.

I lie in bed and stare unseeingly at the ceiling. I'm exhausted and in pain. It's been the same for days: emptiness peppered with unexplained torment. For the most part I feel hollow and lifeless, like I will never experience another positive emotion again, like I must go through the rest of my life with ice for insides. Then, the pain comes. It comes in waves; it wells up inside me without warning, and suddenly it's as if the anguish of every living thing in the world is being fed directly into my mind. I can't stop feeling it, can't stop thinking about how much pain there is in the world—how much suffering, how many sad, unfulfilled, lonely, grieving, dying people there are. But this is just what torments me today. Yesterday, I was treated to a highlight reel of every negative and damaging moment in my own life, and it played on without pause until I was convinced I did not deserve to be alive.

So I begin to fantasize about death again.

I imagine falling off the top of a building, face forwards, arms outstretched. I consider what I'll feel when I hit the ground and for how long I'll feel it. These thoughts come unbidden; my mind always seems to lead me back here when I'm overcome with an episode, as if to test the waters, to test me.

'Maybe this time will be the time,' it says. 'Maybe this time it will finally all be too much.'

I try to contemplate nothingness, try to envision what it would be like to be free of my mind. In the moment it feels like the only way out.

Don't get me wrong, though. I don't want to kill myself. I haven't been actively suicidal for years. It's just that on some days I simply wish I were already dead. I've learned over the years there's a big difference between wishing you were dead and wanting to kill yourself. When I'm in the eye of a particularly fierce emotional storm like this one, I often wish myself out of existence or that I'd never been born at all, but today, I am no closer to killing myself than those without suicidal thoughts are. For me, these thoughts are entirely passive. 'Oh, wouldn't it be lovely if I were dead?' is really a thought akin to, 'Oh, wouldn't it be lovely if I had wings and could fly?' While it's nice to dream of having wings and the freedom they'd allow me, there's absolutely no impetus to actually do anything to change my wing-less state of being.

As Andrew Solomon suggests in The Noonday Demon, yearning to actually take your own life is different. It involves the absence of inertia and a very active struggle towards altering your state of being.

Today is one of those days I dream of having wings. I dream of being carried off to a faraway place where I can finally stop being the living, breathing contradiction that I am—so empty and still so full of pain.

IT'S AS IF MY WRITING IS JOINING IN ON BECOMING A CONSTANT REMINDER THAT I'M SLOWLY UNRAVELLING. THE DATES STEADILY MARCH ON. AN INDICATION THAT THOUGH I AM THE SAME NOTHING ELSE IS. I'M AFRAID OF ALL THAT I WAS BEFORE AND I HAVE TIME STAMPS TO P[...] TIME MARCHES O[...] [...] ITS WAKE MEMORIES. THINGS THAT HAVE SUPPOSEDLY HAPPENED EVEN THOUGH THERE IS NO REAL WAY TO BE SURE IT DID.

I DON'T UNDERSTAND. I STILL DON'T UNDERSTAND AND I'M SO AFRAID. I'M SO AFRAID.

WHY IS THERE NO REASON. WHY ARE WE JUST HERE. WHY IS ANYTHING HERE. I DON'T GET IT. IT MAKES NO SENSE. I DON'T WANT CHILDREN. I CAN'T MAKE SOMETHING WHEN I KNOW IT WILL PERISH. A LIFE. A WHOLE LIFE OF PAIN AND HURT AND FEAR FOR WHAT. TO BE ERASED? SNATCHED OUT OF BEING WITHOUT A WARNING? WHAT IS THE POINT. HOW DOES IT MATTER. SO WHAT IF IT HAPPENED. THOSE ARE JUST CHEMICAL REACTIONS YOU'RE PROGRAMMED TO HAVE. WHAT ARE WE? WHAT AM I?

IS THIS WHY PEOPLE BELIEVE? BECAUSE THE ABSENCE OF AN ANSWER IS SO UNBEARABLE? BECAUSE THE FEAR IS HANGING IN THE AIR? BECAUSE WE'RE A FLUKE? CHANCE. COINCIDENCE? TINY PIECES OF A PUZZLE THAT DOESN'T EVEN COME TOGETHER?

I was born in the late 1980s, the age of dance pop, hoop earrings and pressing questions like, 'Why is everyone's hair so big?' If I am to believe every single account I've ever heard of my birth, I came into this world kicking and screaming, both literally and figuratively, and very much against my will.

My mother laments whenever the story is told. 'You put an end to any romantic notion I had of holding my child for the first time,' she says. 'You were a little, red bundle of fury. You were just so angry that you were here.'

Countless retellings have made one thing abundantly clear. I did not want to be born, and it's a grudge I've seemingly held ever since.

My parents had an unusual courtship, one which was ever-so-slightly complicated by the fact that my father was already married, albeit unhappily, and had

13

two children, my half-siblings Pooja and Rahul. Matters were further complicated by their identities as celebrities. My father, Mahesh Bhatt, was a celebrated film-maker, the director of critically acclaimed films like *Arth* and *Saaransh*, and my mother, Soni Razdan, was an up-and-coming actor. They had a few ups and downs during their secret, four-year-long courtship, but they were imbued with the courage and vitality of love so they persevered. Their arduous journey finally culminated in marriage, and a year later I joined the fray.

The afternoon I was born my father left the hospital for what was supposed to be a few hours on the pretext of making calls to herald my arrival. Instead, he returned at midnight, copiously drunk—he was in the throes of raging alcoholism at the time—and soon found himself at war with the locked nursing home gate. When my mother was informed of his drunken antics, she furiously had my uncle pack him off and get him out of her hair so that she could peacefully sleep off the trauma of birthing an unreasonably unhappy and very uncooperative baby. When my presumably hungover father returned to the nursing home the next day, miraculously he received no punishment. My Teresa-like mother knew there was no point chastising him for something he couldn't control, so she pretended nothing had ever happened and they went back to focusing on their unusually angry newborn.

This has always been the lifeblood of my parents' relationship as well as the essence of who they are. My father is an impulsive, often destructive renegade and my mother is the ultimate stabilizer, a calm and pragmatic port in the storm. These are the two opposing forces that have shaped my life; these are the voices in my head.

Even though I belong to a 'film family' (a rather delightful colloquialism we only seem to use in Bollywood to refer to families who make movies together) there was nothing out of the ordinary about my childhood. Like most other children I knew, I had a conventional, upper-middle-class upbringing. I grew up in a two-bedroom house in the sleepy, tree-lined suburbs of Mumbai with mostly my mother for company. My father was too busy making a living and so he was hardly around when I was a child. Contrary to what people believe, film directors in the '90s didn't exactly break the bank, and even if they did, my father—thanks to his own special brand of masochism—was supporting not one but two families; so while life was always comfortable, it was never lavish.

My father stopped drinking a few days after I was born. He lifted me into his arms one evening and I immediately turned my face away from his (no mean feat considering I was a newborn without fully functioning neck muscles to boast of), repelled by the smell of alcohol on his breath. This rejection from his own child was too much for him to bear and he never touched alcohol again. Once he stopped drinking he didn't really 'socialize' much anymore, neither did he have a large retinue of industry friends, and so, on the whole, my real life (time not spent on movie sets watching him work) from the very beginning had nothing to do with movies.

Despite his newfound sobriety and the overnight annihilation of his social life, my father was still wholly occupied with work. In fact, now, perhaps even more so. He threw himself into his work with even greater gusto and over time, replaced his addiction to alcohol with an addiction to work. So, in these early years, owing to my father's unavoidable absence, my mother and I were a unit. Most of who I was—my blossoming personality, my embryonic worldview—was primarily shaped by her. My father, while hugely influential throughout my later childhood years, was hampered by the limited time he had to spend with me during that period. A lot of the time I had with him was spent on film sets or in music sittings and edit rooms watching him make movies.

Despite all this time spent in close proximity to the film-making process and the odd 'film-child' (heh) friend I had, I was shielded from the Bollywood world.

The fuzzy memories I have of early childhood are all happy ones. I began my education at a small Montessori school not far from home, and once my mother and I made it through a harrowing first week involving a lot of tears, broken promises and her having to sit around directly in Baby Shaheen's eyeline for hours at a time—it was smooth-sailing. Well, for the most part. There was one hysterical temper-tantrum (tiny balled up fists being beaten on the ground, screaming, sobbing, hiccups, the works) thrown in the aisles of a busy supermarket because I was denied a box of crackers, but my mother assures me that that was a one off and not a regular occurrence or some sort of dramatic foreshadowing of things to come.

And then, when I was five years old life changed in an instant, dramatically and forever.

So far, I'd spent my entire life with the undivided, uncontested attention of my mother and those around me, but suddenly there was a tiny new person to share my world with. My sister Alia came into the world during the turbulent 1993 Bombay riots and from the first second I saw her pink, mousey face, life was never the same.

I had desperately wanted a little sister and I was giddy with excitement when Alia was born. She was my pride and joy. Every spare second I had was spent watching over her and playing with her—I soon became so possessive of her that I refused to let anyone else touch her.

Still, adjusting to life with a new sibling is challenging for any young child. As a five-year-old I thrived on being the centre of attention—a stark contrast to the shy and reclusive adult I am now—but the attention that once came solely my way was slowly redirected towards Alia. She was disturbingly cute as a child, and even then she had an effortless knack of drawing people to her. Always the natural performer, most evenings at home involved a spirited performance by Alia to her favourite song of the week, irrespective of whether anyone was watching or not.

My own powers of magnetism, on the other hand, relied more on a carefully crafted combination of jumping, violent arm-waving and incessant demands for people to witness my majesty than effortless charm—and I disliked having to vie for the spotlight.

The contrast in our personalities wasn't as immediately evident when we were younger as it is now, but even though we were both happy, outgoing kids, there were still glimmers of our dissimilarity. Even at that age, Alia was more emotionally self-sufficient than I was. Where I would weep and cry when my mother left me at school or somewhere foreign, Alia would cheerfully wave goodbye without so much as a backward glance. Where I was anxious, restless and seldom able to sit still, Alia was calm and serene. Where I was needy and insecure, she was self-assured and self-contained.

This dissimilitude would get more pronounced as we got older.

Like any child, I was occasionally possessed by bouts of insecurity as a result of this shared landscape, and Alia placidly endured the intermittent bouts of bullying that were borne of that insecurity. I couldn't control the attention that was redirected from me to her, so I controlled her instead, bossing her around like older siblings often do. Sit here, don't sit there, eat your food, give me that, stop singing, say thank you, say please. To this day, a stern, big-sister voice still escapes me if she forgets to say please or thank you to someone while I'm around, and just as she did when she was younger, she serenely and good-naturedly corrects herself.

I loved my sister dearly though and these odd hiccups aside, our childhood was idyllic.

I faced the usual challenges that growing up entails, but all in all, I was a happy, outgoing child and I never lacked love or experienced true discomfort.

But discomfort did come for me, as it unavoidably does in those teenage years.

The aches and pains of growing up began to slowly creep up on me as I got older and steadily became more conscious. But at the start, that's all it really was— discomfort.

My mother always worried that if I went to a posh suburban school I would grow up to be a spoiled, entitled brat (let's just say I was born with a taste for acquisition and the finer things in life. Okay, there was an incident with a Barbie duvet cover in the front of a shop window and some stolen bubblegum, but that's all I am willing to tell), and so when I was eight years old she transferred me to a small Bohri Muslim school in the bustling bylanes of Marol. My school was nothing like the schools the rest of my Juhu friends went to. We wore salwar-kameezes for uniforms, had single divisions with thirty kids to a class (most of whom came from modest backgrounds) and just as it should have been, no one at my school cared what my father did for a living.

For the most part, I truly enjoyed going to school. I was sociable, had a lot of friends, loved my teachers and looked forward to school almost every day. I didn't excel at schoolwork—I had always been a restless and energetic child and focusing on things was a constant challenge—but I did reasonably for my age and I was never really stressed out by school at the start.

The first bouts of discomfort I experienced as a ten year old were caused by run-of-the-mill 'growing up stuff'. It was all a part of the rite of passage we all go through without exception. Doubt and insecurity began to pepper my life. I was suddenly more concerned with the way I looked. I started to compare myself to my peers and worried about my performance at school—all things that were distressing, sure, but not unusual.

But things began to change more profoundly as I approached the age of twelve. I wish I could say there was a specific moment, an instant when everything changed. I rack my mind for the memory of a definitive trigger, the sudden flip of a switch, an inciting incident that led me down this strange emotional path, but there wasn't one. Sometimes I feel as though the change happened overnight, but I know that wasn't the case. I didn't just wake up one morning with my mind fundamentally altered. For me, it happened slowly. It crept up on me one tiny, disconcerting feeling after the other; a lifetime of peace was slowly but still abruptly disrupted by all-encompassing feelings of unease and I couldn't make any sense of it. I was never an exceptional student but suddenly I was struggling at school, a lot more than usual. I couldn't concentrate on much and found myself lapsing into hasty, introspective silences that were difficult to snap out of. It was by no means debilitating, but it felt like a fog was settling over my mind, obscuring my vision and slowing me down.

I had always been a skinny child, the sort of skinny that prompted my mother to ply me with hunger tonics in the hope that I would gain some weight, even though I never did. Suddenly all need for hunger tonics evaporated—all I did was eat. It's true that all growing kids do that, but what I was doing was different. I ate until I was sick, and then I ate more. I would come home from school every day, pile my plate up with a mound of rice and dahi, and eat until I was physically incapable of eating any more. I didn't know what to do with the wave of new feelings that were washing over me, and so I fed them. I fed them until I was roughly the same size and weight as a baby manatee.

It was also around this time, shortly before I turned twelve, that I was made painfully aware of the superficiality and obsession with appearance that consistently seems to contour our day-to-day lives. I was at a precarious age, one at which the seeds of my identity and self-worth were being sown. Up until then, my sense of self had come from my internal make-up and the way in which I interacted with the world around me—exactly as it should have—but all that self-definition was about to undergo surgery.

My half-sister Pooja, who was acting in those days, called one day to invite Alia and me to spend some time with her on-set at an old Pali Hill bungalow while she shot an editorial for the cover of a magazine. Pooja had wanted the photographer to take some personal pictures of the three of us after she was done. She also knew I'd love the visit because the owners of the bungalow had several exotic dogs, including a St Bernard. Even though we'd grown up on film sets, this was a rare and special treat for us; our sister was a star and spending time with her on-set was wildly exciting.

On the day of the shoot we got all dressed up, and I even wore a brand new dress for the occasion. Alia watched Pooja pose for the photographer slack-jawed and in awe while I sat in a corner regarding the St Bernard with the same kind of reverence. When Pooja was done with the last of her shots the photographer summoned Alia and me to join her so that we could take some pictures together. Alia made a beeline for the most prominent spot (obviously) in the foreground of the frame and posed with confidence and flourish, while I hovered nervously and awkwardly behind her.

It was evident I looked distinctly unlike my sisters. Alia was a spitting image of Pooja; they both had light skin, light hair and near-identical features. I, on the other hand, was newly overweight and my already darker skin was tanned from spending too much time in the sun. I looked nothing like them, and I wasn't the only one who noticed. A couple of minutes into the session the photographer turned to me and asked me to step out of the frame. He wanted some shots with just Alia and Pooja.

I feigned nonchalance, smiled, and walked out of the frame without a word.

Behind me everyone 'oohed' and 'aahed' at the cuteness and perfection of this new, Shaheen-less picture. The chorus continued and soon the excited team had whisked my sisters away to a location that better suited their overall adorableness. As they walked away, I wondered if I'd somehow learned to make myself invisible without realizing it. As the minutes wore on it became clear my role in this photoshoot was over, and I spent the rest of my time idly wandering around the bungalow, playing with the dogs and fighting off tears. A few months later those pictures of Alia and Pooja made it into the magazine. There was no mention of me.

As an adult, I can appreciate that experience for what it was: no one present there intended to hurt my feelings, and they were simply responding to a likeness that was right in front of them. As a child, however, all I took away was that I wasn't good enough to be in those photographs. When I went home and looked in the mirror all I saw was a chubby, awkward girl who would never be as beautiful as her older sister or as cute as her younger one. Even at that young age I was already prone to spells of insecurity when I compared myself to Alia. She seemed to flourish with a lot more ease than I did and it made me wonder if I lacked in qualities I should have possessed—and this experience gave my insecurity a whole new dimension. It was also the first time I realized I could be singled out for something I couldn't control—the way I looked, and later, perhaps, the way I felt. It was here, at the age of twelve, that I first began to equate weight with beauty and it was around that time that I first began to peg my self-worth on my physical appearance and compare myself to those around me.

Even today, almost two decades later, looking at those photographs makes me self-conscious and uneasy.

After that disorienting little adventure I decided to take charge of the only aspect of my appearance I had control over: my weight. I became fixated on it. I was already being teased about my weight in school—boys would ask me if I was a bodybuilder because I had a tendency to gain weight on my arms—and I attributed my newfound realizations of distress to this particular, and somewhat physical, wrinkle in my life. Believing that my appearance was the sole cause of all this uneasiness, I began to deprive myself of food to lose weight. I gave my snacks away to friends at school, secretly threw food away at home and went to bed with an empty stomach almost every night. I didn't realize it then, but I had unwittingly kick-started an adverse relationship with food that persists to this day. For months I endlessly obsessed over how I looked, and spent hours crying because I felt ugly and clumsy around other girls my age.

In a short while I managed to lose most of the weight I had gained over the past year and by the time my thirteenth birthday rolled around I had earned the nickname 'sparrow' at school for my sparse eating habits. Finally, my weight was no longer the source of unrest it had been in the months before.

Strangely though, losing weight did nothing to alleviate the feelings of unease I had been struggling with, and contrary to what I thought would happen, the situation only nosedived further. The feelings of sadness and discomfort intensified and I spent nearly every single day constantly on the verge of tears.

I had fixed what I believed to be the problem, but somehow here I was, worse off than when I'd started—unsure and unhappy with the Feeling stubbornly looming over my shoulders.

It's three hours later, and I'm still staring at the ceiling.

It's dark outside now. I know because the shadows on my ceiling have changed shape. The clock has long been ripped from its home on the wall, and it lies face down on the desk with its batteries taken out. Its ceaseless ticking had been driving me further into the arms of madness. I don't need to be reminded of how much time is passing me by, of how much time I'm losing. I feel like I've lost years of my life like this, holed up alone in the darkness. While other people live, I languish within these four walls with all ambition and drive sucked violently out of me. And for what? Most of the time I don't even know. To quote Jonathan Safran Foer from Extremely Loud and Incredibly Close, 'Sometimes I can hear my bones straining under the weight of all the lives I'm not living.'

There is almost never an actual reason for this pain, almost never a concrete, upsetting thought that causes my tears. On the occasion I can say there is, I feel a strange sense of gratitude and relief. I feel lucky on days I actually know why I'm sad. There is deep satisfaction in being able to trace the genesis of a feeling, especially a negative one. When you can identify the source of your sadness, you walk into the feeling armed with an understanding of and familiarity with yourself. Robbed of such cognisance, it's like you're locked out of your own mind—cast out and isolated by even yourself. The rest of the time the anguish is insufferably faceless; a fire that started with no spark. Most days there aren't even tears. On days like that I walk around with a persistent lump in my throat, trying desperately to break through the undetectable veil that seems to keep me separated from the rest of the world, from life.

It still amazes me how well camouflaged it is, this internal maelstrom I'm caught up in. More often than not no one can tell there's anything wrong. Sometimes I wonder if I built and moulded my entire personality in a way that would better help conceal my worst days. I wonder if over time I purposefully grew quiet so people wouldn't notice when I inevitably stopped talking. I wonder if I carefully constructed the reputation of a recluse so they wouldn't be surprised when I disappeared for months on end.

In an instant I'm filled to the brim with familiar self-loathing. Every insecurity I've had as a child and teenager comes roaring back. I hate everything about myself; I hate everything that I am because I am none of the things I should be. I am not kind, intelligent, attractive or interesting. I am even devoid of gratitude from the moral high ground—I've had a near-perfect life bestowed upon me and rather than being thankful, I am tormented.

It's now, in moments like these that I so desperately believe that I'm not supposed to be here, that I was never meant to be born. I know that I don't belong on this planet, because if I did, I would know how to be here. I would know how to be human. I feel like a lost and confused child who is being forced to steer her way through a very adult world. I often wonder if this is what it's going to feel like forever, if I will always see life through this veil of despair, because if this is life, then I don't want it.

My stomach rumbles. I haven't eaten all day, which is highly unusual in the circumstances, food still being my primary form of escapism and self-destruction. It's pretty easy to tell when my mental state is hanging by a thread—just follow the trail of food. I've gained five kilos over the last four months. Things are not as they should be, and my jeans agree.

26.04.2017

DON'T REALLY WANT TO WRITE.
T REALLY. I FEEL JUDGED AND DIRTY AND BROKEN.
HAVEN'T BEEN ABLE TO LEAVE MY ROOM FOR
0 DAYS. I DID TODAY. IT HASN'T HELPED.
WANT TO SEPARATE. TO ISOLATE MYSELF
ROM EVERYONE AROUND ME. I WANT TO
OPPED BEING LOOKED AT.
WANT FREEDOM FROM THE CONCERN OF
PLE. FREEDOM

Teenage Dirtbag

HAVEN'T FELT ~~~~~~ ONG TIME.
IS BROKEN. TH~~~~~~~ HAVEN'T WANTED
T LIKE THIS IN A LONG TIME. I WANT
T RIGHT NOW. NO MORE. NOT ONE MORE
ECOND OF IT. ENOUGH.
WON'T DO IT THOUGH. NEVER.
UT I DO WANT IT. I'M TIRED. TO MY BONES.
F THE WORLD. AND IT'S STANDARDS AND
T'S WAYS AND IT'S NEEDS AND ALL OF IT.
TAKE ME AWAY.

It began slowly—the odd low mood, an occasional barrage of intrusive negative thoughts, a flurry of unexplained tears—but what started out as a flickering flame at a young age was soon a raging wildfire in my teens.

Between the ages of fifteen and nineteen the true onset of my depression collided headlong with a particularly potent dose of teenage angst and it turned my world upside down. I had never experienced pain and sadness of such magnitude before, and I had no reference point for it.

All that uncertainty and unease, that mild discomfort, compounded into an all-encompassing sadness, and my still childlike mind struggled to piece it together.

With this expansive sadness came a predicament, a predicament that made the sadness even harder to shake or ignore. The predicament was this: Sometimes, the sadness didn't feel like sadness at all: it felt like enlightenment.

It felt as though the universe had sighed and unburdened itself of a monumental truth, the weight of which fell squarely on my shoulders. It felt as though I was let in on a secret that no one else knew but me—life is suffering, and there is no point to anything. It was not just that I was lonely. It was that everyone was lonely. It was the sudden realization that I was surrounded by pain, and it was not just my own.

'God, but life is loneliness,' said Sylvia Plath in her journal. 'Despite all the opiates, despite the shrill tinsel gaiety of "parties" with no purpose, despite the false grinning faces we all wear. Yes, there is joy, fulfillment and companionship—but the loneliness of the soul in its appalling self-consciousness is horrible and overpowering.' Suddenly, I was aware of the loneliness of the human condition and there was no unseeing it. I was envious of everyone around me because they seemed blissfully unaware of the world's worst, most inescapable fact: that ultimately, we're all alone and that we're all going to die.

It was an awareness so profound and life-altering that it coloured every experience I had from thereon. Everything began to feel pointless and insignificant— even my own feelings. I was consumed with pain but it didn't matter. Faced with the prospect of my own inevitable annihilation and the annihilation of everyone around me, every emotion I had felt purposeless and irrelevant. What was the point of all this suffering if it didn't actually lead me anywhere? What good is a fleeting life filled with never-ending misery? I soon found myself overcome with an exhaustion so intense that simple everyday tasks became impossible.

I remember standing in front of the bathroom mirror, with my hand hanging limply by my side, fingers wrapped loosely around my toothbrush. I stood there, staring blankly at my own reflection, quietly willing myself to just raise my hand to my mouth and brush my teeth. Not jog 5 km, not hike up a hill, not swim across a river—just brush my teeth, just do something I had done every single day for as long as I could remember.

But, I couldn't. I stood there, as a bit of toothpaste slid off the toothbrush and onto the floor. Plop. I couldn't. I was so tired, so overcome with fatigue that my arms felt like lead. 'What's the point? How does it matter if you brush your teeth or not? How does it matter if you get dressed and go outside? How does it matter if you stay put in front of this mirror for the rest of the day? It doesn't matter.' And so, I stood there unmoving for twenty minutes until I eventually sank to the floor in exhaustion. Then the whole new war to get up and leave the bathroom began.

Like all teenagers I was also prone to yo-yo-ing moods and fits of irrationality, but even then I was acutely aware of the fact that I was having a harder time of it than most people my age. I was crumbling under the weight of self-created expectation. I was never good enough. I continued to do badly at school no matter how hard I tried and sincerely went on to believe I wasn't 'smart' enough. I lived in constant fear of failing all my exams and having to repeat a year while all my friends got promoted and forgot about me. I compared myself to everyone—from my best friend, who was always top of our class, to my little sister, almost six years younger to me, who was rocking the fifth standard better than I ever did. I felt like a failure.

I spent hours staring out of the window, silently wrestling with mounting feelings of hollowness and futility. The only phrase I can conjure up to describe my emotional state during that time is strangely contradictory—I was experiencing a sort of 'hysterical numbness'.

It was like being both dead and alive all at once. It was like a part of me had died and could no longer feel—it could no longer be moved by sight and sound and experience; it could no longer see the value of existing in a living, breathing world.

And it was like another small, immobile part of me was cruelly left alive, condemned to live trapped within the confines of my own unfeeling mind, trapped with the dead part of me, trapped with rot and decay, slowly being poisoned to death. I looked at the world around me and felt an urgent need to escape, to stop. Anything to put an end to this bizarre dance of feeling and not feeling.

The weeks and months I spent doing battle with the Feeling and staving off the belief that I had no real reason to live began to take a higher toll on me. I retreated further and further into myself. My personality had already undergone a considerable amount of change and, as my teenage insecurities grew, I transformed even more.

Two years ago, while Alia and I were in the process of packing up our lives and moving into our own house, I stumbled upon a gold mine—a dusty case of old home movies. Within minutes we were in front of the TV laughing and hooting at the antics of our tiny selves. A seven-year-old me burst into frame, dancing and performing for the camera with, frankly, far too much enthusiasm. 'Darling, do you really have to be in every single shot? We can't see anyone else,' came my mother's patient but weary voice from somewhere off-screen, as I suddenly jumped up in front of the camera, waving at it with a gap-toothed grin and eclipsing everything (i.e., Alia) behind me for the eleventh time in a row.

Present-day Alia turned to look incredulously at present-day me.

'Oh my God! Is this really you?' she said. 'I forgot you used to be like this. What happened to you?'

As I watched the unencumbered, unbridled joy of my younger self, my smile faded and my amusement gave way to a deep, enveloping sadness.

What *did* happen to me? I've been this timid version of myself for so long now that I've forgotten I was ever anything else. I've forgotten that I once used to be free.

My last year at school was full of the emotional turbulences one could expect in those circumstances.

But in my case, I was on one hand being buffeted and tossed around on my troubled inner waters, struggling with ideas of life, death and purpose, and on the other hand I was running as fast as I could, trying to win an external, educational race full of grades, numbers and rankings. I felt nothing but confused and inept.

It was when I was sixteen years old and had somehow, against all odds, made my way into college (my mother cried with joy when I got 73 per cent in my tenth standard board exams, that's how precarious things were) that one of the most damaging elements of my depression—insomnia—made itself known to me for the first time. When you're in the throes of what feels like all-consuming pain, sleep is respite. It's your last refuge from the unrelenting guerrilla attacks carried out against you by your own mind—and here I was, unable to sleep.

Let's get technical for a minute. Very often, insomnia (the inability to fall asleep or stay asleep) and depression go hand in hand, and a disruption of sleep patterns is one of depression's most common symptoms. This disruption doesn't just mean a lack of sleep though; for some people, it can mean sleeping excessively. If it seems odd or surprising to you that a single illness can cause two such contradictory symptoms you've stumbled upon one of the many reasons depression is so complicated to diagnose. Just as there are numerous causes for depression, there are innumerable ways in which it manifests, and some depressives may even experience a yo-yo of sleeping patterns in which they sleep too little on one night and then too much on the next.

While a lack of sleep doesn't always cause depression, there is definitely a link between the two. Sleep is a restorative process, and the human body uses the time in deep slumber to repair itself and carry out functions essential to both our physical and mental well-being. The metabolic waste that we accumulate during waking hours is eliminated during sleep and studies have shown that sleep deprivation impairs everything, from our ability to heal wounds and make memories to the functioning of our immune system. But sleep is still most important for the brain. While our bodies are able to carry out a lot of these healing processes even when awake, our brains aren't, and without enough sleep, our cognitive function becomes severely hampered. Sleep deprivation also diminishes the production of melatonin and serotonin, neurotransmitters that, among other things, help regulate our moods.

The diagnosis of a person suffering from the vicious cycle of both insomnia and depression causes a classic chicken-and-egg problem. After long enough it becomes near impossible to determine whether it's insomnia that's causing the depression or the depression that's causing insomnia.[*]

At the beginning I would toss and turn, wrestling with every negative thought I had while willing myself to fall asleep, though never succeeding. I'd get into bed at night, lie there wide-eyed, exhausted and stirring until morning and then get dressed and leave for college, often subsisting on no more than an hour of sleep each night. This pattern would repeat itself for days, leaving me disoriented, unable to function and almost always sobbing with fatigue. When my mind and body finally crumbled beneath the weight of sleeplessness, I'd drift into fitful, nightmare-ridden sleep, which I sometimes found even less preferable to no sleep at all. Nighttime soon became my personal hell, and I'd be consumed with dread as soon as the sun would set.

[*] https://www.webmd.com/depression/guide/depression-sleep-disorder#1 https://www.psychologytoday.com/gb/blog/the-power-rest/201104/is-depression-making-me-sleepless-or-is-insomnia-making-me-depressed-0https://www.everydayhealth.com/depression/coping-with-depression-and-insomnia.aspx

My quest for a good night's sleep has been one of my most long-fought battles and it was only with the help of medication that I ever felt like I was winning and by the time I was in my late teens I had already become overly dependent on sleep medications and sedatives, without which I couldn't sleep at all.

I eventually gave up trying to sleep on these difficult nights and spent my time finding creative ways to be self-destructive instead. I discovered alcohol when I was sixteen years old. I discovered it like most teenagers do, with friends, and like most of the lot, we spent an inordinate amount of time chasing its highs. I loved how alcohol made me feel. It was an instant tranquillizer, making me blissfully numb to the flood of bad feelings I was otherwise unable to contain. I soon discovered that if I drank enough, I could impose on myself the lack of consciousness I so desperately craved.

Binge drinking wasn't a big deal when I was a teenager because everyone else my age was doing it too. We all got carried away with the newfound freedom of college under the illusion of finally being adults. All sleepovers at friends' homes involved stealing alcohol from the bars of their slumbering, blissfully oblivious parents. All socializing came with the pursuit of alcohol and getting into clubs.

But the numbing effects of alcohol didn't last long—the more I drank, the less it helped, and ultimately it began to exacerbate my pain instead of dulling it. I have an oddly (odd because of the sheer amount I had had to drink that night) vivid memory from when I was seventeen years old and I got into a rather serious spot of trouble with my mother for coming home drunk one evening. I had stumbled home, quite obviously trashed, way past my ten o'clock curfew after an evening involving one too many beers with my friends. Now, the average Indian mother, as any Indian child knows only too well, possesses the well-honed ability to provoke nightmares with no more than a deliberate narrowing of the eyes. They're terrifying enough on a normal day when the full extent of your wrongdoings are things like talking on the phone three minutes past your bedtime or having to explain why and how you've already run out of your weekly allowance on Thursday. So, you can imagine that in the event that you do something that doesn't just violate totally arbitrary (yeah that's right, Mom) mom laws but is *actually* dangerous and bad for you, that ability to induce terror takes on an entirely new dimension. Suffice to say, what was awaiting me when I got home was . . . not pretty.

The resulting blowout involved all the usual things you would expect in a situation like this. There was, understandably, a lot of screaming, a lot of tears, a fair number of threats and a rather sizeable loss of future freedoms and liberty. But, for the first time on my part, there was also a brief moment of complete honesty. In my less inhibited, liquored-up state, as my mother yelled at me, the words that I still remember so clearly, came bursting out of me before I could stop them.

'Mama, I feel so empty. Why do I feel so empty?' And that was it. I spent the next hour heaving with drunken sobs with my head on my mother's lap, repeating the same words back to her every five minutes as she gently and worriedly stroked my head to calm me down. The next day, she was obviously intent on discussing my mini-meltdown from the night before but, now that the tongue-loosening effects of alcohol had worn off, I was back to being my tight-lipped, evasive self. I somehow managed to talk my way out of discussing what I had said in great detail, and succeeded in assuring her that I was fine and that I was overstating how I felt because of the alcohol and thankfully, she let it go.

It was only when I was in my twenties and the novelty of alcohol had all but worn off that I realized I used alcohol as a crutch during depressive episodes. I wasn't an alcoholic; I could stop drinking for months at a time when I chose to, but I had my alcoholic father's genes, and every time my mood plummeted my abuse of alcohol soared.

In the times I drank to escape, I did it to hide from my feelings because it was too agonizing to confront them.

It took me years to learn that no matter how hard I tried, I couldn't outrun my feelings and the antidote to them definitely wasn't at the bottom of a bottle. Even today, drinking and partying requires constant self-restraint and is no longer an option when my mood is low.

Depression and substance abuse form a cycle according to Andrew Solomon, author of *The Noonday Demon* and a long-time sufferer of depression, who you will find me quote a lot throughout this book. People who are depressed abuse substances in an attempt to free themselves of depression, and in doing so damage their lives to the extent that they become further depressed by the wear-and-tear their abusive behaviour causes.

I've found that for me this abuse isn't restricted to substances like alcohol alone. I'm an emotional eater and my relationship with food, much like my relationship with myself, is a troubled one. It is said that most addictive behaviours are caused by underlying mental and emotional issues. When you're depressed or anxious you're desperate to feel good, or at the very least desperate to feel less bad. In order to avoid feelings of stress and sadness we turn to not-so-great things that will help us feel better; things like alcohol, unhealthy food and binge-watching *Keeping Up with the Kardashians.*

My relationship with food and my body soured at the onset of my depression when I was eleven years old and it never quite recovered.

For most young girls, insecurities and self-esteem issues caused by poor or problematic body image are inevitable and form a part of growing up and learning how to be comfortable in your own skin. At a young age I formed lasting mental and emotional associations between my weight and the idea of happiness and it's something I'm certain a lot of us do.

Since that time, my weight has fluctuated wildly, unhealthily, and almost yearly. Just like with alcohol, when my mood plummets, the amount of food on my plate skyrockets. I eat without love or enjoyment, and I eat compulsively. For over fifteen years I have oscillated between bouts of binge eating and deprivation and I honestly can't remember the last time I ate normally.

Writing the first version of this book took a heavy toll on me. The process involved venturing back into emotional pits I had long clambered out of and once there, I stayed. Unsurprisingly, I fell back on some well-tested, destructive coping mechanisms and in the six months it took me to write the book I gained over ten kilos.

This has been the story of most of my life. When I'm free of the Feeling, my self-image is positive and I'm able to nurture myself and keep myself healthy. But when the Feeling is present, it is swiftly followed by an overwhelming narrative of futility which obscures all good judgement, leaving me unable to look after myself.

And so, when I was younger, my weight and the way I looked was a constant source of medical and cosmetic concern and a fairly accurate gauge of how I was doing emotionally.

My worried parents had long realized that something was wrong with me in those teenage years, even though, like me, they didn't quite know what the problem was. I had slowly walled myself off to greater and greater degrees until there came a point where I would no longer leave my room. What eventually emerged was more surly panda—I had dark circles down to my toes—than secretive teenager. My mother was disturbed by how much of a misanthropic loner I was growing to be and she, like me, was reaching a breaking point. About five times a day she would come hammering on my door yelling at me to leave my bedroom while I either yelled back or ignored her entirely. To her mind I was simply a lazy, detached, rude teenager. I could hardly blame her for feeling that way because many times I wondered if I was those things too. I wondered if I was just spoiled and unambitious, content with living out my life within the four walls of my bedroom because I didn't want to make an effort. By this point my education had more or less come to a standstill. I had chosen to attend college in Bombay over a prestigious IB school outside the city because the anxiety of leaving home was more than I could bear.

Lost in an overcrowded system where most students were faceless and there was no real accountability, I barely attended classes and spent all my time holed up at home or out with my friends. Often, I would leave the house, make the effort to travel the one-hour distance to college but then change my mind at the last minute and not attend lectures after all. After the academic struggle that was the end of my school life, I became indifferent towards my continued education. It was too much work and I was quite certain that I would never pursue a career that required a degree, so I just gave up.

Teenagers are incredibly innovative when it comes to hiding things from their parents, and they're also frighteningly good at it. No matter how well you think you know your teenage child, or their various exploits, trust me, what you know is only the tip of the iceberg. I was blessed with open-minded and liberal parents and I rarely had cause to lie to them. As a result, they were more aware of my escapades than most of my friends' parents were of their children. Despite their understanding and my mother's hawk-like attention to my life, I had managed to carefully hide away a whole distorted inner world that I didn't allow them access to. This left them with no other option but to discipline my wayward ways as best they could, and while it did keep me out of trouble, they were unable to figure out the driving force behind this quiet rebellion, concealed as it was.

Truly, I was ashamed and afraid of how I felt. I hadn't yet come to terms with my feelings and to tell my parents about them would be to admit they were real and I was too weak to deal with them on my own. It took a much darker phase in my life for me to finally admit that I needed help.

If someone were standing outside my bedroom right now with their ear pressed against the door they would mostly hear the hum of silence.

But, if they were the sort of person who really enjoyed standing around outside people's bedroom doors listening for noises and they hung around long enough, every few minutes they might hear something like:

'Ugh, shut up' or 'Stop it, just stop it' or 'La la la la la la la I can't hear you'.

Upon hearing this they might infer that I'm having a distressingly childish argument with someone on the telephone, but they would be wrong.

In actuality, what I'm doing is lying flat in bed surfing the Internet with my laptop on my chest, yelling at myself every few minutes for no apparent reason.

Depression, when combined with a good broadband connection allows for a lot of time to learn things, I'll admit. In the past hour I've learned a great deal about penguins, the commonness of homosexuality in the animal kingdom, Sjogren's Syndrome, Spontaneous Human Combustion, the fall of Pompeii, super-volcanoes and the Greek origins of common English words. Did you know the word 'telephone' comes from the Greek words for sound (phon) and far away (tele)? You didn't? Well, now you do.

I've also been reading a lot about shame.

You know shame . . . it's that thing that makes you feel like your brain is suddenly dissolving, melting through the base of your skull and emptying out into your stomach, collecting in a lead-like ball at the bottom of your abdomen that threatens to pull you deep down into the ground, but no matter how far down it pulls you, it won't be enough because nothing, not even being vapourized by the earth's molten outer core, is enough to help you forget and escape the intense, all-consuming humiliation and embarrassment of simply being you.

That shame.

I've received many explanations and theories for why I suffer from the crippling and intense feelings of shame that I experience almost every other day during a steady month and every other second during a not-so-steady month. Anxiety, melodrama, overthinking, low self-esteem, bad upbringing, masochism, narcissism, fatalism, being human: these are just some of the theories that have been so helpfully proposed.

I don't know what it is. I don't know if these feelings of shame are the crux of depression or if they're just one small facet of the disorder.

I don't know whether it's depression that causes shame or whether people who experience more shame are more susceptible to depression. What I do know that somehow most people who live with depression, live with some sort of shame.

Whether it's shame about who you are: I'm not good enough, smart enough, successful enough, pretty enough, thin enough.

Shame about what depression has turned you into: I'm not productive enough, reliable enough, happy enough.

Shame about being depressed at all: I'm not normal enough.

Shame about not being able to control all these disturbing thoughts: I'm not enough.

Convincing you that you're a vile, loathsome creature not worthy of the existence that has been bestowed upon you—that's one of depression's many specialties.

For me, even a feeling as common as embarrassment is usually enough to send me into an immobilizing shame spiral. I've always had high levels of social anxiety (also an offshoot of shame) and I've always been incredibly awkward in social situations. People I'm unfamiliar with make me nervous. I either make too much eye contact or too little, I find even regular small talk challenging, I say all the wrong things, become cripplingly self-conscious and basically just freeze. The pressure to be 'cool' and unruffled is always infinitely higher in situations where you don't know people very well, and there's nothing quite as uncool as someone trying really hard to be cool.

Sure, saying something stupid to someone at a party a long time ago may not seem monumental enough to cause the sort of crippling low-level shame (also known as 'OhMyGodWhatIsWRONGWithME' syndrome) that makes you wish you were dead, but like I said, this is one of depression's specialties. It takes a should-be-simple and common enough feeling like embarrassment then shakes it, blends it and churns it until it goes deeper than the simple act of doing or saying something stupid.

You've said something stupid because you are stupid.

You're worthless. You don't know how to behave normally or talk to people.

You're fat, you're ugly, you're not even good at your job.

And, everyone sees it. They look at you and think you're an idiotic waste of space.

They laugh at you behind your back. Just like you've always suspected.

You're useless and broken and can't be fixed.

You should do the world a favour and just disappear.

That. That's shame.

Embarrassment while similar to shame, is still very different. Embarrassment is situational and occurs when the image you want to project to the world takes a hit and there are spectators.

Like when you're doing your cool walk and someone sees you trip over your own foot. That's embarrassing.

Shame, on the other hand, is the all-pervasive feeling that there is something fundamentally wrong with who you are. It's what makes you want to hide. It's what makes you want to isolate yourself, to vanish from the world so that no one will notice all the horrible things about you that you know to be true.

Shame and guilt are not the same either. Guilt can often be a positive emotion that helps you alter your behaviour—if you believe you have behaved badly—and it pushes you to behave more morally in the future.

Guilt is all about making amends while shame is about hiding, isolating and escaping.

You experience guilt when you do something bad. You experience shame when you believe you are bad. There's *nothing more toxic or more distressing than believing that the problem, the root cause of everything wrong with your life and everything you are, is you. What do you even do with that? How do you fix who you are?*

In a bid to postpone having to come up with an answer to that rather terrifying question I decided to do a little digging and understand the destructive emotion traipsing around in my head. I learned a lot, and of the things I learned, here's what I found particularly interesting about shame: it's a social emotion. As it turns out, the entire purpose of shame and the reason it exists at all, is to control and regulate human behaviour. In the two-hundred-thousand odd years that we've been around, human beings have essentially evolved as pack animals who both lived and hunted in large groups. In order for these large packs to flourish and succeed, they needed to all work together for food and protection. Strong social relationships were not only critical to the survival of the group at large but also pertinent to the individual, who relied on these relationships, to sustain oneself.

'In this world, your life depended on others valuing you enough to give you and your children food, protection, and care. The more you are valued by the individuals with whom you live—as a cooperative partner, potential mate, skilled

hunter, formidable ally, trustworthy friend, helpful relative, dangerous enemy—the more weight they will put on your welfare in making decisions. You will be helped more and harmed less,' says John Tooby, a professor of anthropology at UC Santa Barbara.

We may not be hunter-gatherers any more, but human beings have banded together on a scale like no other species before us. Through the use of language and emotion, seven billion of us, spread all across the globe, have learned to work towards one common goal—the progress and evolution of the human race. This gargantuan feat would not be possible without somehow being able to keep individual behaviour in check on a large scale to ensure everyone is following a prescribed and beneficial path, and that's where shame comes in.

Biologically and historically speaking, the function of shame is to prevent you from exhibiting behaviour that is perceived as wrong or dangerous by the group at large— behaviour that could cause setbacks to all this progress we have made or put the survival of the pack in jeopardy. It also exists to keep your social relationships intact by ensuring you don't damage them with harmful behaviour—all to give you the highest chance at survival. Essentially, shame causes you psychological pain so that you can see mistakes that you're making and correct yourself.

Correct yourself. As you can see shame functions on the principle that both you and your behaviour are fundamentally incorrect. While shame does serve a function, (it's also what prevents people from causing each other grievous harm) there is a point at which shame becomes toxic. Certainly, most people dealing with mood or anxiety disorders seem to have an overdeveloped ability to feel shame.

It's fascinating to me how depression both fuels shame and feeds off of it. Like with the other existential facets of depression, it's a mystifying chicken-and-egg situation. What came first, the shame or the depression?

I have had intense feelings of shame since I was a teenager, and it's only recently that I was able to identify all the horrible voices in my head as the toxic voices of shame.

That humiliating moment at the photoshoot in my childhood triggered an explosion of shame that centred around my appearance. Since that moment I have spent my entire life trying to 'fix' the way I look. That shame is what has often been the reason I've had more to fix than I otherwise would have. The more shame I felt about my appearance, the more I ate to feel better and the worse my circumstances became.

Depression and the lethargy it caused robbed me of my will and ability to be productive or feel like I was contributing to society, and that in turn led to deep feelings of shame about my value as a person. From there on I have lived through a vicious cycle of shame and painful, hurtful feelings, one feeding off the other in an endless loop.

For the past hour, every humiliating, shame-inducing moment in my life has been having a leisurely walkabout through my mind. For the past hour, I've tried to occupy my mind as best I can in a bid to prevent myself from jumping out of the window, hence the gathering of useless but oddly fitting scraps of information——like, the 'mare' part of the word nightmare comes from Germanic folklore where 'mare' is an evil female spirit or goblin that sits upon a sleeping person's chest, suffocating them and/or giving them bad dreams.

I've also been yelling at my own head whenever it throws up a particularly painful memory, hence the seemingly insane, unprovoked bouts of shouting.

Maybe I'm not depressed at all.

Maybe I'm just a shitty person.

Maybe I just hate myself and call it depression.

Maybe this is all my fault.

Maybe I should be ashamed of myself.

legible | handwriting | 10+

IS WRITING SUPPOSED TO BE THIS DIFFI
ALWAYS CAME SO NATURALLY TO ME.
WHAT I WOULD WRITE. THOUGHTS POP
EASE. THIS FEELS STUPID TO ME NOW.
LIFE IS SO TERRIBLY TRIVIAL, AND I'M
IT IMPORTANCE AND INJECT THE IDEA
AND PHILOSOPHICAL FLAIR.

A LOT HAS CHANGED SINCE I LAST PUT
HAS CHANGED. I'M OLDER, ALL OF 21
MUCH WISER, I'M CALMER? AND IF IT'S
AND MORE CONFUSED THAN I WAS AT 16
I FOUND OUT THERE'S AN ACTUAL MEDIC
UNEXPLAINED PAIN, SUFFERING AND SELF
I HAVE NOW GOT THREE CATS LIVING
JOY IN THE OCEAN OF MISERY AND H
I'M MORE OVERWEIGHT AND LOWER ON
AND FINALLY, MY ONLY SUBJECT OF THOU
IT'S ALL I THINK ABOUT. EVERY DAY. EVER
TIME NO LONGER MEANS ANYTHING. ONE
BE GONE. SO WILL EVERYONE I LOVE. THIS
POINTLESS.

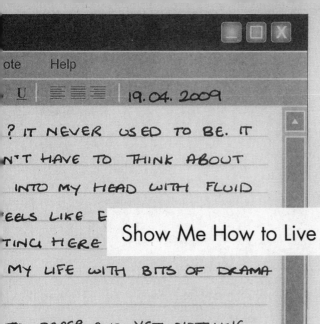

ote Help

U ≡ ≡ ≡ 19.04.2009

? IT NEVER USED TO BE. IT
N'T HAVE TO THINK ABOUT
 INTO MY HEAD WITH FLUID
EELS LIKE E   Show Me How to Live
TING HERE
 MY LIFE WITH BITS OF DRAMA

 TO PAPER, AND YET NOTHING
S 143 DAYS OLDER, I'M NOT
SIBLE, I'M SADDER, MORE ALONE

CAUSE FOR MY CONSTANT AND
THING.
 ME, THE ONLY DROP OF
LIATION THAT IS MY LIFE.
LF-BELIEF.
 IS THE SAME: DEATH.
UR. EVERY MINUTE. EVERY SECOND
Y I WILL
T IS   Are you sure you want
            to continue ?

> ▮ ◀ 14:21 flick here to continue

Nestled inconspicuously in the back of my first journal (a ruled Navneet long-book that was originally a maths workbook, easily repurposed by tearing out the first five pages) in a messy, inconsistent scrawl, is my first (yes, there would be others) suicide note.

In it, I bid farewell to my best friend. The note contains only the briefest explanation of my state of mind. It seems she already knew enough of how rough a time I'd been having because it didn't warrant more clarification. The bulk of the note comprises instructions: don't cry for me, always be happy, and always love boys (sigh, in my feeble defence we were teenagers and boys took up a significant amount of mental processor power at the time. Things are different now.)

(Okay, fine, that's a lie, things are pretty much the same.)

This is the earliest mention of suicide I can find in my journals, and mortifying contents aside, that note is very solid proof of how far down the emotional rabbit hole I was so early on.

I was fourteen years old.

I was introduced to the notion of suicide in a magazine article that detailed the experiences of a twenty-year-old girl who took her own life, and once the idea had been instilled in me, I fixated on it. Looking back, now I know my preoccupation with the idea came from an irresponsible reportage in which suicide was romanticized. The article suggested that the young girl, whose life had ended tragically and prematurely, was now free. It subtly condoned the act by presenting it alongside a positive idea, when the truth is, suicide is not the path to freedom and liberation, rather the end of all freedom.

At fourteen I lacked even the most basic understanding of the implications and finality of death, and so I was incapable of grasping what it actually meant to even contemplate suicide, let alone go through with it. With my limited understanding of death at that time, I began to see suicide as a route to relief. The pain I was dealing with, while terrible, had not yet scaled the dizzying heights it would in the years to come. At fourteen, suicide was nothing more than an intellectually appealing solution to my emotional problems. It almost seemed like a logical fix—I wouldn't feel pain if I didn't exist.

However, my perception of suicide slowly changed as I got older and the effects of depression intensified.

It was November 2004. I had just visited a couple of friends in Mahim and I hopped on to the local train to Virar to make my way back home. It was 3 o'clock in the afternoon and the compartment was all but empty. Even though it was the end of November, it was an unusually muggy day. I stood alone at the entrance of the second-class compartment, staring out, entranced by the train tracks as they flew past me in a blur of rust-red colour.

It was a short journey home and I had only one thought as the train barrelled down its route: to throw myself out of the compartment. I remember the little voice in my head that egged me on. 'Just jump,' it said. 'Jump and it will be over. Jump and you don't have to go one more second feeling like this.' I stood there in a daze until suddenly I looked up and saw the sign that read Andheri. In all my suicidal contemplations, I had missed my stop.

With what felt like enormous difficulty, I heaved myself off the train, not onto the tracks as I'd been so convinced I should, but onto the platform, and I made the now slightly longer auto ride home.

It was my sixteenth birthday.

As the pain and hollowness within me mounted it became more and more unbearable and suicide was no longer just an idea, no longer just a potential solution that was waiting to be picked off the shelf. It soon became vital and necessary. No longer a choice but an inevitability.

My notions and understanding of death also changed as I witnessed it more closely and suffered the gut-wrenching consequences of it.

When I was sixteen years old, Alia and I had a caretaker, Sharda, who was like an older sister and friend to us. She had come to live with us shortly before my tenth birthday and as a result was a part of some of the most important and impressionable years of my life. She was a part of our family and she cared for us like we were her own. She knew almost everything about me—what food I liked, what scared me, which boy I had a crush on. We laughed, we fought, we even shared a room.

Sharda died unexpectedly in a road accident one humid August evening. She was twenty-eight.

I will never forget the moment I found out about her death. My father's words still ring in my head. 'How do I prepare you for bad news?' he asked me gravely on the phone. The absurdity of it all sunk in then. 'I'll be fine . . . you can tell me,' I said, trying hard to control my voice from trembling. 'She's dead.' I heard him say, after what felt like eternity. All my senses felt numb, my heart started pounding. I tried to keep my cool until I hung up. 'I'll be fine, Papa,' I said. My voice was quivering. I sat staring into nothingness for five whole minutes before I realized what had just happened. I could feel my entire body rejecting the idea of the truth I had just heard. My head started screaming at me . . . all I could see was her face, all I could hear was her voice. Sounds rushed past my ears making absolutely no sense. I wanted to scream, I wanted to shout . . . I wanted to do so many things. Instead, I just cried.

Going home after the knowledge of what happened was the scariest thing I had to do. I felt blinded with the intensity of the emotions that hit me then. I found it hard to breathe. The idea that she wasn't coming back the next day seemed bizarre. I opened her cupboard only to find a photograph of her, which was taken merely five months ago. It was at that moment, that very moment when I realized she was never coming back. Not to wake me up in the morning, not to yell at me for leaving my clothes on the floor, not to make sure I ate my dinner.

Stunned by this encounter with the after-effects of death, it was the first time I came face-to-face with the irreversible finality of someone simply ceasing to be. All of a sudden, this person, who was such a huge part of our lives, was gone forever and no amount of bargaining or wishful thinking would ever bring her back. It crushed me. In our family I took the news of her death the hardest.

I plunged further into the far reaches of my depressive hole and by this time (as a result of both the unescapable natural progression of my invisible illness as well as this horrific experience) the romantic and conceptual notions of death and suicide I once had—that it was my one path to salvation—had faded away. To me there was nothing beautiful or romantic about it. I saw it as the irreversible end of being that it was and I witnessed and experienced the insurmountable pain that the living who were left behind were so cruelly condemned to.

I saw death for what it was and I was terrified of it.

And still, in the face of all this learning, understanding and fear, death was all that was left for me.

All my idealistic notions had been replaced with despair, a gut-wrenching feeling that I was left with no other means of escape. I was barely sleeping and no matter how much time I spent doing things I loved or hanging out with my friends and family, I would always come back to the same dark, unrelenting, painful place in my mind. My moods had begun to border on hysteria, and I felt like I was trapped in a life I had no idea how to live. Now in my first year pursuing a bachelor's degree in literature and psychology, I was attending classes even less frequently than before. Eventually, my college could no longer overlook my lack of attendance and I was understandably asked to leave. I had no option but to continue to pursue my degree through distance learning, but that meant a lot more time at home doing nothing, and a lot more time with my increasingly murky thoughts.

A few years ago, I came across this passage in David Foster Wallace's seminal novel *Infinite Jest* and nothing sums up my feelings in those days more aptly than this:

[The] 'psychotically depressed' person who tries to kill herself doesn't do so out of 'hopelessness' . . . not because death seems suddenly appealing. The person . . . will kill herself the same way a trapped person will eventually jump from the window of a burning high-rise . . . Their terror of falling from a great height is still just as great as it would be for you or me . . . The variable here is the other terror, the fire's flames: when the flames get close enough, falling to death becomes the slightly less terrible of two terrors.

Like Wallace describes I was trapped in my own mind, and while the prospect of death was still terrifying, it wasn't half as terrifying as the thought of being imprisoned by this pain forever.

It was 2006, and I felt I had finally reached the end of my already frayed tether.

No longer able to grapple with the seemingly unending pain inside me, I swallowed a bunch of Tylenol PM in my bathroom when no one was home, and made a feeble attempt to take my own life. The human body is a wondrous thing and the pills combined with the undiluted, courage-bolstering Vodka I washed my pills down with, made me sick enough to throw up. A few hours, some throwing up and rather a lot of disorientation later, it was like my body, fed up with what my mind had almost cost us both, decided to zap some clarity into me.

The sheer desperation of that moment was like a painfully overdue electric shock. It led me to the understanding that this was no longer something that I could safely keep to myself. I realized that I was dealing with something far beyond my control. It took a moment of staring into the abyss for me to concede and acknowledge that I needed serious help, and faced with the potential irreversibility of my actions, I was finally driven to confess the truth of my inner world to my mother.

Suicide is a notoriously permanent solution to a vacillating problem. As Andrew Solomon in *The Noonday Demon* observes, when depressive episodes come, it feels as though they will never leave, but that is rarely ever the case. A person experiencing their first depressive episode is more likely to attempt suicide, while someone who has lived through a few episodes has more or less learned how to cope with them, and more importantly recognized that they eventually end. My previous belief that I could never find respite was the driving force behind my suicidal thoughts and tendencies in my late teens. I hadn't had the time or—infuriating as this word is to a teenager—experience to ask and answer vital questions about death and suicide that I needed to, but once I did, I was able to see the holes in the reasoning that had led me down the path in the first place.

'It is impossible to know the consequences of suicide until one has undertaken it,' says Andrew Solomon. 'To travel to the other side of death on a return ticket is an attractive idea: I have often wanted to kill myself for a month. One shrinks from the apparent finality of death . . . Consciousness makes us human, and there seems to be general agreement that consciousness as we know it is unlikely to exist beyond death, that the curiosity we would satisfy will not exist by the time it is answered. When I have wished to be dead and wondered what it would be like to be dead, I have also recognized that to be dead would defeat the wondering.'

I'd been morbidly fixated on death and the idea of taking my own life since I was fourteen years old but after that experience, the thought of suicide left me, and it was replaced with an all-consuming terror of death.

The awareness I achieved as a result of my suicidal contemplations—of the inevitability of death and its irrevocable conclusiveness—sent me flying in the other direction so much so now death is always at the back of my mind. Saying this, I wish it were an exaggeration, but it isn't. I spend the majority of my days actively pushing this fear away so that I can get on with actually living my life. I walk around with a tiny voice in my head, a voice I've rather transparently and ham-fistedly named Syl, after Sylvia Plath. Syl is always there to remind me that death is coming for me and everyone around me. Syl lurks in the shadowy parts of my mind, keeping up a running commentary that centres around my impending annihilation.

When the Feeling gains control so does Syl, and I can't drown her out. When I'm steady, I do everything I can to muffle her nihilistic voice with my own life-affirming one. I fill my head and heart with as much positive noise as I can in a bid to make her quiet. But at times I can't escape the stark and inexorable facts of life Syl constantly reminds me of, no matter what I do. There are days on which life will do Syl's job for her and show me through example that death is everywhere, and usually it's on days like these that you'll find me curled up crying on my bathroom floor.

I still have days on which I wish that I simply did not exist. I have days on which I wish I had never been born, I have days on which I wish I would die in my sleep. I even have really bad days on which thoughts of suicide start to waft about inside my head again. I have these thoughts, but right now, I also have a kind of certainty that I will never act on them.

It seems absurd to me now that I ever seriously contemplated suicide, that I ever thought of hastening this inevitability I'm so horrified by. Time that's passing me by is time I'm losing, and I'm terrified at the thought of my own end, especially since every moment is inching closer and closer to it. Every happy spell in my life is contaminated with the knowledge of how fleeting such moments are, and so most of my life is spent trying to disentangle this contingency from the moment at hand.

To forget.

To escape.

I wonder when I'll learn that just like feelings, there are some things you simply can't outrun.

It's the dead of night and I've been tossing and turning, drifting in and out of broken sleep.

In the few barely conscious, wakeful seconds I take to turn over, a little voice in my head pipes up out of nowhere. 'You're going to die one day,' it says, as if it's been patiently cradling this little nugget of truth all night and waiting for the perfect opportunity to hurl it at me. In an instant my stomach drops and my eyes fly wide open in the dark. I'm taken by fear.

I'm wide awake now, my heart still pounding. I grit my teeth in frustration. There seems to be no end to the number of ways in which my mind chooses to disrupt my life. You'd think it would be on my side. But no, it's just one truth bomb after another with the stupid thing.

In time my fear of death combined with pre-existing health conditions have given rise to a very inconvenient bout of health anxiety. When the anxiety is at its peak I can't go anywhere that's more than fifteen minutes away from a hospital, convinced as I am that I'm going to have a sudden medical emergency and drop dead. There is, of course, no reasoning with my stubborn mind and it refuses to listen to reason and accept that vaguely healthy thirty-somethings don't just cease to exist for no reason. This fear is so great that I even carry around inhalers for asthma I don't actually have. The idiocy of this isn't lost on me. Some days I feel like I ought to be shrunk down and studied under a microscope.

I curl up and close my eyes, trying to push the thought of death out of my mind. It won't budge. Soon my thoughts have spiralled downwards. I'm thinking about all those I've lost to death and all those I'm still to lose. It's like a film of horrific hypotheticals playing on loop in my mind.

Thoughts like these would usually send me into a fit of tears but it's been two weeks of this misery and I think my tear ducts have had quite enough and gone on strike.

Sleep is a distant memory now. I heave myself out of bed and trudge to the kitchen to make myself a cup of cocoa. Several minutes later I'm seated at the window sill in the living room, cocoa in hand, silently watching the velvety night sky lighten as the house sighs with sleep.

I haven't realized it yet but this is the first time I've left my bedroom in a week.

13TH JUNE 2014

PEN TO PAPER. NOTHING TO SAY.

ORDS LOSE MORE MEANING EVERYDAY. I BARELY FEEL ANYMORE.
HEN IT ALL HURTS HOW DO YOU DIFFERENCIATE BETWEEN A
EELING? WHEN IT'S ALWAYS DARK HOW DOES IT MATTER IF THE SUN
AS RISEN?

Y HEART IS HEAVY WITH THE PAIN OF THOSE WHO WERE BEFORE ME.
CRUMBLES UNDER THE WEIGHT OF THE STREAM OF FEAR THAT HAS
D NO BEGINNING AND WILL HAVE NO END. THE FUTILITY OF A
ATING HEART. THE POINTLESSNESS OF LOVE.
N, LOSS, FEAR, GRIEF, CHANGE — THE ONLY CONSTANTS IN AN
STEADY WORLD. DESTRUCTION.
HY DOES NO ONE TELL Y   ATION MEANS DESTRUCTION?
HEN YOU AGREE TO CREAT   O DESTROY.
D ONE EVER MENTIONS

Crawling

DON'T KNOW WHY I GOT TO BE HERE.
DON'T KNOW HOW TO MAKE IT STOP.
DON'T KNOW HOW TO HELP.
UCK LOVE. FUCK LOSS. FUCK LIFE.
NFINITY ALLOWS FOR INFINITE ENDS.
T FEELS LIKE I END EVERY SINGLE DAY.

∞ ∞ ∞

31ST AUGUST 2015

Y PEN IS BLEEDING INK. MY PEN, IS BLEEDING.
AVE APPEARED TO HAVE STUMBLED UPON A TRAGIC FACT OF LIFE.
U RUN AND YOU RUN TO END UP WHERE YOU STARTED.
HY DO PEOPLE TRY TO TELL YOU SELF-WORTH IS AN INTERNAL
NSTRUCT OR STATE? I HAVEN'T MET A SINGLE PERSON WHOSE
NSE OF SELF DIDN'T COME FROM EXTERNAL VALIDATION? LOGIC
CTATES THAT YOUR WORTH IS DETERMINED BY THE VALUE OTHER
OPLE SEE IN YOU. HOW DOES IT MATTER WHAT YOU'RE SELLING IF
ONE WANTS TO BUY IT?
M WHAT I AM. AND NO BODY IS BUYING.
EEL LIKE A FRAUD. A FACADE WITH NO INTERIOR.
CONSTANTLY CLOAKED IN FEAR I WEAR IT LIKE A PRIZE.
WONDER NO ONE'S BUYING. I HAVE NOTHING TO SELL.
TIGUE HAS SET IN. DEEP, ENVELOPING FATIGUE.
N MANY TIMES MUST I TRY TO BECOME ANOTHER AND FAIL?

I had my first panic attack when I was eighteen years old, post TylenolGate, while getting a hair cut.

In general I've always found salons to be unnecessarily stressful and anxiety-provoking places. Every person who works at a salon is effortlessly outgoing, dresses like they've jumped right off the page of some cool, hipster fashion magazine, and has the sort of flawless hairstyle that only Greek gods could pull off. Maybe years of salon-xiety (a genuine and should-seriously-be-recognized condition caused by feeling dangerously uncool whenever you are at or in the vicinity of a salon) finally took its toll on me, and I snapped. Maybe the overwhelming smell of hydrogen peroxide sent my central nervous system into a tizzy. Maybe having to sit still in one place for so long while someone tutted at my lack of hair care ritual awoke my claustrophobia. Honestly, I don't know what made it happen or why, all I know is that I was suddenly sure I was going to die. As I looked in the mirror (already an unpleasant enough experience when your hair is wet, clipped above your head in five different places and poking out at weird angles causing your face to look like a giant squishy bao bun [every girl on earth knows what I'm talking about]) I experienced several wildly uncomfortable sensations, all at the same time.

First, my heart felt like it had suddenly and suicidally nosedived directly into my stomach while pumping at a ridiculous 600 beats per minute.

Second, every inch of my body instantly went cold and numb, as if its blood supply was cut off and its every nerve ending had malfunctioned and died.

Third, I developed a terrible case of tunnel vision and was disoriented by how everything was simultaneously in front of me but not at all in front of me.

Fourth, my entire experience of reality changed. In a moment I felt completely removed from my own body. I felt as though the invisible connection between mind and body had been completely severed and I was hovering somewhere outside of myself, a disembodied tangle of thoughts with the fast fading memory of the word 'I' trying to hold it all together.

Fifth, my brain started screaming at me 'Oh my God, you're going crazy. Oh my God, you're dying! You're having a heart attack! Human hearts are not built to beat this fast! You can't breathe! Your throat is closing! You're having an allergic reaction to this haircut! Of course you can have an allergic reaction to a haircut, you're just the first person to ever have one!'

My body tensed up and froze as all these alarming new physical sensations rose, and crashed and cascaded over me.

By now the chic, muscular, pierced and tattooed man cutting my hair had noticed something was going on with me because I was rather conspicuously staring at my own reflection in the mirror with my eyes widened in horror and my mouth hanging open in a sort of silent scream.

'All good?' he cautiously ventured.

My eyes slowly shifted from my own face up to his and with the same wide-eyed horror I somehow hoarsely breathed the words, 'YesI'mfinethankyouthisisgoinggreatcanIhave aglassofwaterpleaseIneedtogotothebathroom,' abruptly stood up, scarpered to the bathroom and then barricaded myself in.

Ten minutes later I managed to pull myself together long enough to finish the haircut teetering between the belief that I was either losing my mind or dying. As soon as I was done, I hightailed it over to the doctor to make sure that I hadn't arrived at the tragic, would-be-widely-reported, end of my young life.

It turns out, deep emotional scarring aside, there was nothing physically wrong with me. I still didn't realize what I had experienced was a panic attack though, so I continued to be convinced that I was grievously ill.

That first attack kick-started a spate of anxiety-related symptoms that I have battled with ever since and I still haven't managed to resolve. After getting the boot from college in 2006, my life was in flux. I was getting my degree, sure, but I didn't have classes to attend and it was mostly because my mother refused to even entertain the possibility that I might not finish school. With no real external pressure or sense of purpose I slid further into a life of inaction. This continued for the next two years in varying degrees and even after I finally got my degree a life of nothing became normal and 'something' became increasingly harder to pursue. All my pursuits came in non-committal bursts and my productivity waxed and waned with my moods. I'd work on a script for two months then do nothing for four, I'd do a short course in editing then fall back into a depressive slump locking myself in my bedroom for a month, and on and on it went. My day-to-day life comprised of a steady, unchanging stream of guilt and anxiety, guilt for never doing as much as I should have and the constant anxiety that I was steadily losing more and more time. And the anxiety never abated.

I had several more panic attacks after that first one, one of which took place when I was due to get back on a flight home from a holiday in Bangkok. I still have the ID card from the hospital visit as a fond and funny memento. Every time someone wants to know what a panic attack looks like I show them that ID card. In it, is the expression I so intimately got to know while looking at myself in the mirror during that first panic attack—eyes widened in horror, mouth open in a silent scream. I also (less fondly) remember the alarm in my mother's voice when I called her from the hospital, hyperventilating, to inform her that I would not be getting on the flight back home and that Thailand was my home now.

I was convinced that once I got on that plane and was thirty-five-thousand feet in the air, somewhere over the Bay of Bengal, I would have a heart attack and die. So, I resolved to stay in the hospital until I could be certain that my heart was not about to give up on me and just stop beating. A few hours, a consultation with one Dr Spain and some potent anti-anxiety medication later, I did get on the plane but I spent all six hours in near tears, breathing into a bag while maintaining a vice-like grip on the armrest.

Health anxiety was and still is one of the most debilitating side effects of depression I've experienced. My fixation on death and my all-consuming fear of it, was the perfect fuel for this anxious, hypochondriac fire. It doesn't help that I have had notoriously bad luck with my health either.

Now, every time I go somewhere new or unfamiliar I do a quick Google search for the nearest hospital. Every time I'm in a darkened theatre or auditorium, I sit in an aisle seat so I can leave immediately if I need to. Before I get on a plane I make sure I have a goodbye letter written just in case. I also carry around a pouch of medication with me everywhere I go. It contains everything from anti-allergy and anti-anxiety medications to bronchodilators and medication to lower my heart rate. I've never had to use most of the contents in that pouch. But I have them all, just in case.

'Just in case' and 'what if'—the taglines for anxiety.

Of course, anxiety isn't limited to panic attacks and hypochondria. There are many different kinds of anxiety disorders. Anxiety disorders are mental disorders that have anxiety and fear as their primary characteristics. Put simply, fear is a response to current, stressful or disturbing events while anxiety is worry about possible future events.

Generalized Anxiety Disorder, Panic Disorder, Social Anxiety, Post-traumatic Stress Disorder (PTSD), Obsessive Compulsive Disorder and Agoraphobia are just some of the types of anxiety.

I also have terrible social anxiety. Shocking, I know. The list never ends.

Being around unfamiliar people is hard for me. Being around large groups of people is hard for me. Being in situations where I'm the focus (I hate birthdays so so much) is hard for me.

The family I come from is a confident one. My parents, my siblings—they're self-assured and they're poised.

I'm not like that.

I'm awkward (read: downright stupid) in social situations, I don't make much eye contact, I talk too fast, I say the wrong things (Them: Nice to meet you; Me: You're welcome; Them: Happy Birthday; Me: You too), I shrink.

I'm notorious for never responding to text messages or answering the phone or going to places I'm invited to and I have literally ducked behind things in public places to avoid saying hello to old acquaintances.

It took me a long time to realize that anxiety has taken over my life almost as much as depression has.

I've heard a lot of people say that if given a choice, they would take the certainty of depression over the uncertainty of anxiety a thousand times over . . . and, I kind of get why.

Anxiety and depression make strange but inseparable bedfellows (I've always wanted to use that expression).

Inseparable, because depression and anxiety frequently exist side by side. Depression can cause anxiety and flipped the other way around, anxiety can cause depression. They coexist, though that isn't necessarily always the case.

Strange, because depression and anxiety are fundamentally conflicting experiences.

Say what you will about depression, but it's not uncertain about what it wants you to feel. It's not unsure. It's single-minded and blinkered in its vision for you, the host, and it expertly executes its masterplan. When you are depressed, you don't question the futility of life. It just is futile. You're not unsure about whether the future is bleak and hopeless or not. You know it is hopeless, it's a fact. You aren't doubtful about whether or not you're going to get better. You simply aren't. It's impossible.

Depression is futility brought to life and given a home inside your mind.

Anxiety is the complete opposite. It is uncertainty. It is the fear that something bad might be coming if you aren't fully prepared.

It is worrying that things are different than they seem. That people who say they like you don't actually like you. That the same cheque you've deposited month after month isn't going to clear. That the niggling itch in your throat is something much worse than a cough. That everything you think you know is a lie.

With anxiety, your life is a carefully constructed pyramid of playing cards that is always a light breeze away from collapsing (or well, fluttering) to the ground.

When you're depressed, time stops.

When you're anxious, it speeds up in a terrifying, unsettling and inconsistent way.

Depression is lying immobile on the ground for hours.

Anxiety is fidgeting, pacing and hyperventilating.

Depression is grief.

Anxiety is fear.

A mind experiencing depression and anxiety side by side is like the unfortunate piece of rope caught in a game of tug of war. It's constantly being pulled and tugged and stretched in opposite directions with no respite. The second you settle into a feeling, another contradictory one comes along and takes its place. And on and on it goes until your brain is reduced to a puddle of mush. For me, depression at its worst is like being cold and still and dead. Anxiety is like having a mind that's on fire and being charred to ash. It's what makes the day-to-day awkwardness of being me unbearable, as if it wasn't already hard enough.

Something under my left knee buzzes.

Closer inspection reveals it's my phone again.

Seven missed calls and three trillion messages.

This time it's my mother.

'How are you feeling?' the message reads.

I told her on day two of this episode that I wasn't feeling well. Migraine, I think I said. It's the easiest thing to fake if someone comes over unannounced. You don't have all that pretend coughing and sniffling to contend with.

All these years later, I still do it, I still instinctively brush past and hide my worst days.

Especially from my family.

I know how much they worry, and I know how helpless they feel when they can't help.

I'm grateful for how much they care and I'm grateful for the fact that I have the comfort and luxury of a supportive, loving family. But on days like this, even a simple 'How are you feeling' is an impossible question to answer. Even the concern from my loved ones is draining. I feel compelled to reassure other people that I'm okay because if I don't they'll spend their time trying to make me feel better or asking me questions I don't have the energy to answer.

So sometimes, I just say I'm sick. Or don't respond at all.

I glance through the rest of my messages. More of the same.

'Tried calling, call me when you're free.'

'Dude, are we still on for tomorrow?'

'Are you hibernating again?'

Most people in my life exhibit remarkable patience with me.

I've spent years swinging wildly between being an attentive friend who's all there and being absent, unreliable and distracted.

Isolation is one of the hallmarks of depression.

The shame and the fatigue of depression are just a few of the many reasons I find that I tend to isolate myself. For me, some of the most alienating and exhausting parts of this entire experience come from simply having to explain to people how I feel.

It always seems like an exercise in futility.

I could never string together the right sequence of words to sufficiently describe the sheer chaos of the tempest raging in my head.

And I can hardly respond to 'How are you feeling?' with 'Not so great, there's a tempest raging in my head' every single time.

So instead, I say, 'Not so great, I have a headache.'

At least when I say I have a headache the looks of commiseration I get are straightforward. Everyone understands what it's like to have a headache. Everyone's had a headache before and even if they haven't it's easy enough to say 'Well, it sorta feels like someone's repeatedly stabbing me with a small fork right here, behind my left eye.'

'Ahhh, oh nooo, those are the worst,' they'll say with their brows furrowed in sympathy before they reliably offer up their own foolproof headache cures.

A raging tempest is a little harder to describe without risking the chance of being met with looks of polite confusion, blankness or that face someone makes when trying to do a complicated division sum in their head without breaking eye contact.

On days like today I don't have the wherewithal to explain the tempest so, I just brush over it.

I respond to my mother.

'Headache better. Still not 100%. Hopefully tomorrow will be better.'

N,

How u doin?

Good i hope.

Gosh I'm gonna miss you.

You really are my best friend.

Do me a favo̶u̶r̶ ̶.̶.̶.̶ ̶n̶ ever cry for me.

Promse me th̶a̶t̶ ̶i̶f̶ ̶u̶ ever do i'll take

it as an insult to my memory and come

haunt you. In a good way though

so at least we can still do things

together.

I'm gonna try talkin to my mom or

try therapy, but if that doesn't work

here's some advice for life

① Follow your heart

② Always love boys

③ Never beat yourself up about a guy

EVER.

④ Get rid of your braces

⑤ STUDY! 96% in you boards okay?

⑥ Don't forget me.

⑦ Get a boyfriend.

Always with you - your buddy

Shaheen

Depression world over is almost exclusively described through the use of metaphors, analogies and symbolism.

The only descriptive words we have to try and communicate pain—words like 'sadness' and 'grief'—don't even begin to reveal the complexity of the emotions they're assigned to. It's why we must resort to likening depression to parasitic monsters that drain us of our joy or dark shadows that consume us.

'No one understands how I feel' is in all probability the most frequently thought and spoken descriptor of depression (and being a teenager) of all time, and I think that's because it's true. No one can truly understand how you feel because the pain you experience is unique to you. Negative emotions draw deeply from who you are and your unrepeatable set of experiences and insecurities, which is why they're so different for everyone. Your mind's every response is a product of experiences that are yours alone and pain routinely taps into every single one of them. It takes your whole life, and every single incidence and coincidence that has ever happened to you, to make you who you are. Every cut, every scrape, every hurtful word, every heartbreak, every good or bad thing you have ever done, every mistake you have ever made and so much more come together to make you the beautiful, complex, perfectly messy creature you currently are, and it is precisely this self-definition that makes sadness such a solitary and isolating emotion. Your pain, like your fingerprints, is unique to you.

In other words, you can buy happiness off the rack— but sadness is tailor-made just for you.

When describing our emotions words can only take us so far, yet words are all we have. So often the problem isn't with the emotions themselves but the language we use to describe them. The drawback of using language as much as we do—as our dominant method of interaction with the world, those around us and even ourselves—is that we sometimes forget how limited the code of language is. Sadness is not created, encoded, stored and decoded in language alone, yet language is the only vessel through which we can communicate it, providing us with only the barest representation of our feelings.

Think about the word 'hot' for a second. Think about reaching your hand out towards the flickering flame of a candle. Think about the rapid changes in sensation you experience as you get closer and closer to the light—how the warmth is pleasant and spreads through your fingers and down your hand as you approach the halo of the flame, how the sensation intensifies and escalates meteorically with every passing nanosecond, how before you've had the chance to register and assimilate the satisfying part of the experience that enjoyable warmth has been replaced by a vague discomfort and a mounting sensation of burning until, in an instant, you snap your hand away from the flame and cradle your fingers in your other, more temperate hand, shooting a nasty look at the tiny little flame that wanted nothing to do with you in the first place.

Now consider how effectively the word 'hot' describes such a discovery and understanding of the state of the flame.

So, how effectively can any word we make up describe the throbbing, consuming ache of sadness and pain?

I think, the reason depression is so misunderstood is that there is no truly adequate way to relay what it feels like. It's why the only people who really understand it are those who've experienced it firsthand, and even then, their experience of it may differ greatly from your own.

This is why I sometimes wonder if words are where it all went wrong.

Human beings created language, and to distil light years of semantic theory, we used that language to identify a feeling and give it a name.

If we strip all of it away—the words, the constructs and concepts of mental illness—or the boxes we create to slot and control, what are we left with?

A feeling. A feeling that expresses itself as a series of questions: Who am I? Why am I here? What is life? Why am I alive? I didn't ask to be born, why do I have to die?

Over time and generations these questions have come to be rote, but cliches are cliches for a reason. It is upon the bedrock of these very questions that the human consciousness is built and everything we do in life is an attempt to answer them, to explain our state of being and come to terms with the perturbing inevitability of our ceasing to exist one day. Yet, faced with a lack of clarity to these impossible questions we never really answer them; so we choose to forget instead. We neatly tuck the questions away or find resolution through faith and get on with our lives because that's all we can do if we want to live lives that are not bogged down by fears we have no way of assuaging. It's why so many of us shy away from talking about the unresolvable predicaments of life—death, depression, feelings. With the absence of concrete answers we simply choose to move on with our lives rather than painfully ponder the questions, and we make peace with not knowing or fully understanding the circumstances of our existence.

I sometimes wonder if my only problem is that I have a constant and more acute awareness of the impermanence of the world around me, a visceral link to the laws governing my life. Man-made laws, to a certain extent, I can control. Physical laws I can't—and perhaps it's from this helplessness that my issues stem. Maybe cognizance is my only problem.

I don't mean to suggest that others without depression are less cognizant or self-aware, but perhaps they possess a more refined ability to tune out this awareness and get on with their lives. Maybe it's just that the depressed find it harder to ignore reminders of the transience of life in everything that surrounds us. Maybe all we see is a flashing neon sign that reads 'futile'.

'It is this acute awareness of transience and limitation that constitutes mild depression,' says Andrew Solomon in *The Noonday Demon*. Is that true? Is that what depression really is? Think, to be bogged down by a fear of impermanence in a world that isn't a permanent place to begin with. Then how does my place in the world matter? Why agonize over my purpose in life when both life and purpose are fleeting?

Maybe all I possess is a big-picture vantage point that I'm unable to clamber down from. The world around me is being put into constant, unfiltered perspective, and while others can push it away and forget about it, I can't.

Maybe my only problem is that I'm one of those who can't forget.

Hey all,

I dunno when you're reading this, but whenever it is, I'm wondering where I am as much as you are. This is not a suicide note.

It's just a note to say I'm sorry and don't blame yourselves.

Spoonful of Sugar

Through all the silent and occasionally not-so-silent struggles in my teenage years, my mother had been hard-pressed trying to help me in spite of not knowing what the problem was. And all I did was shut her out and pretend I was fine. She'd nudge me gently, suggest I see a psychiatrist or psychotherapist often enough, but I'd aggressively shoot down her advice each and every time. She could see I was struggling but I had expertly concealed the worst of it from her and she didn't really realize the full extent of what I was grappling with. But, in the aftermath of swallowing those pills, I knew that had to change.

A few days after the Tylenol incident I sat down with my mother and slowly and shakily attempted to unburden myself of the mountainous load I had been carrying all on my own.

'Something's wrong, Mama, I feel empty,' I remember mumbling to her.

It was a glaring summer afternoon and she was in the living room, busy paying bills.

I had been sitting across from her, wrestling with my thoughts in silence for almost fifteen minutes before I finally got the words out.

'Hmmm, what darling?' she asked absentmindedly.

'I feel empty. I feel so empty that it hurts.'

She looked up at me, bills forgotten. 'Okay, in what way exactly?' she asked slowly, looking concerned.

'I don't know,' I said, still not properly meeting her gaze. 'I just feel . . . wrong.'

A tear trickled down my face, uninvited. This was the first time I had ever tried to articulate what it was that I had been feeling for all this time. For six years the Feeling had slowly taken root in me and mounted and escalated and finally led me to this moment. It was the first time I had ever really acknowledged, even to myself, that something was wrong . . . and I had no way of describing it.

'I'm not happy. I can't remember the last time I was happy. I can't remember the last time I wasn't this sad. Everything hurts. It hurts all the time and I'm scared I'll never stop feeling like this. I'm really scared.'

I didn't exactly tell her what had prompted this long, overdue confession—I was too afraid that she would never let me out of her sight again if I told her—but I said everything I could to make her aware of the gravity of the situation I had found myself in.

She listened quietly as I continued talking, her face growing from concerned to resolute. When I was done she held me in her arms and reassured me in the way that only mothers can. 'Don't worry. I love you and we're going to figure out what's going on and deal with it together,' she said.

If you're anything like me, you'll scoff at the idea that a stranger can teach you things about yourself that you don't already know. But as human beings we're full of unconscious motivations and historical explanations for our current patterns of behaviour. Psychotherapy, or talk therapy, is the first line of defence against mental illness, and it provides a non-judgemental environment in which you can share your thoughts and feelings and feel supported and understood. Some forms of therapy are insight-oriented and help increase your self-awareness, while other forms offer specific, research-based techniques to help you challenge your negative thinking, manage stress, improve your mood and enhance the quality of your relationships. Psychotherapists are usually able to provide you with guidance and help you ascertain whether or not you're in need of further medical intervention and are required to progress to the second line of defence—meeting with a psychiatrist.

The difference between psychotherapists, psychologists and psychiatrists is often a source of confusion for people.

To put it simply, a psychologist is someone who has a PhD in psychology, while psychotherapist is an umbrella term used to describe a professional who treats emotional issues—psychotherapists can include psychologists but they can also include trained therapists who do not hold a doctorate and are equipped to provide counselling and guidance at a graduate level. Both focus on treatment involving psychotherapy and behavioural interventions.

Neither psychologists nor psychotherapists are able to prescribe medication, however—this is a qualification possessed by psychiatrists who are trained medical doctors, and who focus primarily on treatment through medication.

For me, given the precarious mental place I was in at the time, meeting a psychiatrist was no longer *an* option, it was the *only* option. My mother had understood the pain I was in, and while she recognized whatever I was grappling with was not to be taken lightly, she knew it was not for her to decide what was going on with me. The very next day I was in the waiting room, nervously readying myself for my first therapy session.

The road to a diagnosis began there. I was ordered to do a series of blood tests which revealed that among other things, I had extremely low levels of serotonin,

Me (aged 3) looking confused on Papa's film set, 1990

Alia and Pooja: the picture of Alia and Pooja that made it to
the magazine on the day of that fateful photoshoot, 1998

Mummy, Papa and I, the cute baby, shortly after I was born,
1987 or 1988

Me, Mummy and Papa on my third birthday (what on earth is that dress?), 1990

Alia (aged 3) and I (aged 8) chowing down on some mangoes, 1996

Baby Alia and I, 1993

Papa, Alia and I the day she came home from the hospital, 1993

Me (aged 11) bemusedly watching Alia put stickers all over her face for reasons known only to her at her sixth birthday party

Alia feeding Papa cake at her fourth birthday party; me (aged 9, in more questionable clothing) looking on

Papa no doubt telling me (aged 14) about the secret meaning
of life in the middle of a party

Me (aged 7) showing off some sweet ballet
moves and a gap-toothed smile

Alia and I (finally well dressed) at an event in 2016

Alia and I channeling our inner mallards in her vanity
van, 2016

Mummy, Papa, Alia and I during a family vacation in
the Maldives, 2016

Alia, Mum and I, 2017

a neurotransmitter considered one of the primary contributors to feelings of well-being and happiness. Further sessions of psychoanalysis, therapy and psychological testing confirmed I was dealing with major depressive disorder and soon enough, I started on medication to help alleviate the severity of my symptoms.

There is still a lot of debate, controversy and conjecture about the diagnostic tools and treatments available for depression and other mental health illnesses. There are a lot of studies that link low levels of serotonin to depression but there are an equal number of studies that suggest that serotonin's role in depression has been, at the very least, largely exaggerated.

There are a lot of people who claim that medication has helped cure them of depressive and other symptoms, but, there are just as many who claim it hasn't helped them, or, in some cases, has made them worse. While modern psychiatry is perhaps a lot further along than it was twenty years ago, the fact remains that there is still a whole lot we simply don't know.

To begin with, we still lack a complete and exhaustive understanding of the brain—the alleged birthplace of all mental illness. We don't even understand where consciousness—the source of every existential idea—comes from.

We struggle with the very basics—what qualifies as depression in the first place? All our treatments are based on the idea that there exists a fundamental imbalance in the mind, but, in order to define the parameters of what constitutes an *imbalance*, you must first understand what *balance* is. In order to pinpoint what abnormal is, you must first define normal. If there is such a thing as ideal brain chemistry we are yet to define it. If there is such a thing as ideal emotional state we are also yet to define that.

To this day, despite the many purported causes for mental illness, there has been no way to conclusively link depression to any one cause. According to a piece published by Harvard Medical School, 'It's often said that depression results from a chemical imbalance, but that . . . doesn't capture how complex the disease is.' It goes on to say that 'depression doesn't spring from simply having too much or too little of certain brain chemicals. Rather, there are many possible causes of depression, including faulty mood regulation by the brain, genetic vulnerability, stressful life events, medications, and medical problems . . .

'To be sure, chemicals are involved in this process, but it is not a simple matter of one chemical being too low and another too high. Rather, many chemicals are involved, working both inside and outside nerve cells.'[+]

[+] https://www.health.harvard.edu/mind-and-mood/what-causes-depression

Given that there is no concrete or absolute cause for depression yet, there is also no one, foolproof way to diagnose it. There is no simple blood test or X-Ray to pinpoint the causes of depression or mental illness, instead as psychiatrist Allen Frances puts it 'psychiatric diagnosis still relies exclusively on fallible subjective judgements rather than objective biological tests'. As a result of all this diagnostic ambiguity there is no one treatment for mental illness either, and psychiatrists can't always predict which treatments will work and for whom. Does that mean treatments don't work? No, it doesn't. It just means that what constitutes 'treatment' looks different for everyone.

While there *have* been a lot of advancements in what we've learned about the biology of depression we're still a long way from seeing the whole picture. We are in the early days still, the middle ages of psychiatric science, in the sense that there are numerous treatment options available to choose from but figuring out what works still involves a lot of hunches and guesswork. Psychiatrists and psychotherapists have to play the part of both medical professionals as well as detectives. They have to work to untangle and ascertain not only the possible biological causes of a mental illness but also the unique psychological causes of one. As a result, individual treatment plans take work and patience to find and perfect. It means a willingness to accept that what worked for someone else may not necessarily work for you, and vice versa. It means that no one treatment is a magic cure-all.

Keeping in mind that that information we have is still somewhat incomplete, we must educate ourselves to the best of our ability and use whatever tools we have available to us to begin to form a clearer picture.

I can't say I took to therapy easily or that I was thrilled about being branded mentally ill and needing anti-depressants, but I had finally understood what I was going through was much bigger than me, and that I had to try everything I could to feel like 'myself' again. For me, I found that both talk therapy and specific medication did work to improve my state of mind, but, even then my depression was not miraculously cured and some of my worst years were still to come. But within a year of that frightened attempt at suicide I had gotten to a place where all *active* desire to end my life left me, and so far, it hasn't come back.

As a teenager, I hadn't yet learned I could help myself with the right tools like talk therapy, medication and exercise and, most importantly, had the realization that relief could be achieved at all. I also didn't realize the effect being a teenager was having on my depression. Our bodies experience an extraordinary number of chemical changes through puberty. We're flooded with hormones that affect our moods, which have a marked effect on our neurochemistry. Whether you're depressed or not and whether you're prone to mental illness or not, being a teenager involves developmental turmoil. It took the settling down of all these chemical reactions in my body to finally allow me the chance to accurately assess my situation for the first time.

By the time I was in my early twenties, therapists and psychiatrists had become a regular fixture in my life. I learned early on in the experience that finding the right therapist, like finding the right relationship, can take a great deal of patience and willingness to occasionally be disappointed. We're all built differently, and we all respond uniquely to various forms of care. All psychotherapists and psychiatrists have their own personalities and varied approaches to healing, and therapy is most successful when you find someone you can communicate well with. I'll be honest, the first therapist I went to was not a good fit for me at all. She was a psychiatrist who also offered counselling, and talk therapy was obviously not her field of expertise. She also always had a waiting room full of people making the process both long and extremely rushed, so she wasn't able to give me the care or the attention I needed at the time. I went to several before I settled on one who suited me, and once I found a rhythm and established a good relationship with my therapist, I found the experience to be invaluable. I believe that for me, depression started out as something that had a chemical trigger, but because I lived with it for so many years at such a sensitive time in my life—my teenage years—it progressively became more and more psychological. Therapy taught me so much about myself and my psychological triggers and defences. It helped me delve deep into my fears and insecurities and gave me a deeper understanding of where they came from. I learned to spot and identify all the ways in which I unknowingly hampered my own progress. Years of living with depression had given rise to a number of unconscious behaviours that acted as defence mechanisms and they, as much as the illness itself, were also holding me back. It was through therapy that I realized how much shame and self-loathing I had cultivated over the years. I didn't just not like myself, I *hated* myself. And there was no pill to pop for that.

Therapy is nothing but an education in yourself; an opportunity to elevate the way you live your life. I'd recommend therapy to anyone, not just someone who lives with mental illness.

I faced a similar struggle with accepting medication. I was afraid of the implications, but in retrospect I realize that my personal aversion to medication was a pre-conditioned response that came from ignorance and misinformation about anti-depressants. It took a lot of experimentation with medication for me to find the ones that suited me. Some made me feel dull or sleepy or tired, others made me feel bloated and uncomfortable and hungry, still others made me feel no different at all. With trial and error, I found the medication and doses that worked for me and still allowed me to feel like myself. I learned that my moods could be regulated and I didn't have to go through the rest of my life feeling so bleak and devoid of hope. It wasn't a miraculous solution that fixed me overnight. Anti-depressants don't make you giddy with joy and happiness, and they definitely don't cause a 'high' like numerous people believe. Anti-depressants simply make you . . . less sad. They make your moods and your pain manageable, getting you to a steady enough emotional state to allow you to start implementing treatments and working on the things that need work. It helps make depression feel like a controllable challenge rather than something dark and unbeatable.

However, in dealing with depression, further cures are necessary. I had taken the first steps towards healing myself, but I still struggled with being labelled 'depressed', and in particular its characterization as a mental illness.

I grappled with what it meant for me and for my identity to be branded as someone who had a mental illness. It was already incredibly difficult to confess to the magnitude of my sadness, but once the tag was added to the mix, it seemed to get even harder. Being diagnosed wasn't as straightforward as just accepting the label.

On one hand, there was a huge sense of relief in finally having a name for the thing I had been battling with for so long. There was also relief in being able to look at my mum and my friends and go, 'Aha! SEE. I wasn't just being lazy and spoiled and difficult. How stupid do you feel now?'

But, on the other hand, there was also a ton of denial.

The negative voices of depression that lived in my head for so long had done a very thorough job with me and they had convinced me that I was just crazy and no good.

'Depressed' just sounded like far too convenient an answer—it almost felt like a way out—a nice way to convince myself that I wasn't as worthless as I felt.

There was also a marked difference in the way I thought I was perceived when I told people I was clinically depressed. When I was sad, I was just sad—I was someone who was struggling under the weight of difficulties life was throwing at me. But when I was depressed, I was either damaged or a drama queen— there was something fundamentally wrong with my make-up as a person.

While people's reactions were varied, for the most part they contained nuggets of either fear or scepticism.

They were either unwilling to believe I was depressed, preferring to look at me as someone who was lazy and melodramatic, and if they did believe me, they saw me as someone who wasn't entirely stable. Even then I knew that caution and apprehension were natural reactions to things that are not fully understood, but it was difficult not to take these reactions at least a little personally, especially when they came from 'adults'.

It was my father who taught me a long time ago that no one can disrespect you or shame you without your permission. When I was eight years old I came home crying from school one day because a classmate had called me stupid after I failed a maths test.

'First, there's nothing wrong with being stupid. I'm stupid,' I remember my father saying, talking loudly and patiently to be heard over the sound of my furious, rather theatrical sobs. 'Only stupid people can learn things, *beta*. Smart people think they already know everything.'

'But I'm *not* stupid, Papa,' I moaned, tears streaming down my face.

'Then what's the problem?' he shot back. 'If someone calls you stupid and you are stupid, then it shouldn't bother you because what they're saying is true, and if someone calls you stupid and you aren't stupid, then also it shouldn't bother you because what they're saying is not true. Neither the truth nor lies should trouble you.'

That lesson has stayed with me my entire life and it's what came back to me during those days when I was first learning to cope with people's reactions to my condition. People labelling me depressed needn't have bothered me because it was the truth, and people construing there was something wrong with me as a result of my being depressed or calling me crazy or a drama queen needn't have bothered me either because that wasn't the truth—and deep down inside I already knew that. I had to take the power out of the words people were using and put more power into what I was telling myself.

The reactions I got weren't all negative, however. I also received an overwhelming amount of love and patience from those close to me. Even if they didn't understand what I was going through they made every effort so I would feel safe and loved. And in the midst of their care and understanding, I began to notice the effect my depression was, in turn, having on them. I had spent years gazing intently inwards; I hadn't stopped to consider how my ups and downs impacted other people.

My own relationships suffered because I lacked an awareness of my actions. My moods were constantly waxing and waning, and when there were downs, my predominant coping mechanism was to shut down completely. From my very first depressive episode I both consciously and unconsciously shut out the people who were nearest to me. Like so many depressives, I cloaked myself in silence. 'Shame unravels human connection,' says Dr Brene Brown and nothing could be more true. All the shame I felt deep down inside caused me to shut down, to hide, to stifle my voice. My family and friends suffered at the hands of my brooding silences, and my romantic relationships suffered in a myriad of other ways. I was unable to talk about how I felt and the few times I was, I didn't believe the people I loved were strong enough to hear and contain what I had to say. For me, my inability to communicate was one of my biggest hurdles.

By the time I was in my early twenties, depression had made me bitter and angry. Years of wrestling with my moods had taken their toll, and I had almost come to resent people who were capable of being happy. It had negatively impacted everything in my life from my health (I was always ill and suffered from chronic pain) to my pursuit of a career, and I was sick of it. My pain slowly began to twist and contort into rage. Everything made me angry. I was angry about how I felt, about how little control I seemed to have over my own mind. I was angry about the choices I had made because of how I felt. I was angry about how I was floundering while everyone around me was succeeding. Worst of all I was angry because no matter how angry I was about the state of my life and no matter how much I wanted it to be different I just couldn't make the change happen. I was angry about who I was, and I took it out on the people I loved.

In its worst moments, depression affects your ability to love as well as to be loved, leaving you incapable of either. So it's hardly surprising that some of depression's greatest damage is in the realm of relationships. While the psychological and emotional wear-and-tear that depression causes is palpable, the hushed, corrosive effect it has on relationships might not be as obvious at first. I've lived with depression for all my adult life, but it's only now, almost twenty years in, that I've begun to understand what depression means *to* me and *for* me. It's taken all these years' worth of depressive episodes to become familiar with the particular texture of my sadness. The mistakes I've made and the hard-won truths I've learned, I did so the difficult way—through relentless experience.

Before these lessons I was often oblivious to a very simple fact: the person living with depression is not the only one who suffers at its hands. Every family member, romantic partner and close friend suffers too. I've said this before, and I'll say it again, living with depression isn't easy but loving someone who lives with depression isn't easy either. It's challenging enough to live with a depressive person who has learned how to navigate their episodes and has understood the impact they can have, but living with someone who does not understand what is happening to them is a whole other type of challenge.

Depression is such an internal and solitary process that try as you might there is no way of truly explaining what it feels like and the fact of the matter is aside from providing you with love and understanding, there's not much anyone close to you can do to help you through it. The snag is that relationships in general, even the ones that don't have mental illness to contend with, are notoriously burdened with unrealistic expectations when it comes to understanding and problem-solving. You believe that the other person should 'just know' exactly what you're going through while the other person believes it is their responsibility to help you feel better . . . but they often can't. The truth is someone is never going to fully understand how you feel unless they've been through the same thing (sometimes not even then, and they're certainly not going to understand if you don't explain it to them), and it is not their responsibility to cure you of your sadness. And that's okay—it's a survivable reality—but it's a reality that takes time and effort to come to terms with.

Over time, I came up with a very basic rule for when I'm depressed. The rule is that when I feel an episode coming on or when I am in the throes of one, I say it. I tell my loved ones that I'm sad. I let them know my sadness is not in any way because of them and I assure them that if I need help, I will ask for it. For me, this simple step of taking the guesswork out of the process has made a tremendous difference and has significantly improved the quality of my relationships during tough times.

I'm silent but the screaming wont
stop.
I'm calm but the restlessness goes
on.
I'm ~~smiling~~ but my frown wont
fade **Break Stuff**
I'm laughing but the tears dont
die away.
I'm living but that wont stop
death from coming my way.

The way I see it, it was the phase of anger in my depression—not the phase of suicidal ideation—that was my rock bottom. I say this because this was the point at which I lost sight of who I was. This was the point at which the empathy I believe defines me as a person was obscured by anger and frustration.

I couldn't help how I felt, and I had learned it wasn't my fault I felt the way I did, but I had also learned neither was it anyone else's. While I had begun to see how difficult it was for others to cope with my depression, I didn't know where to begin taking responsibility for myself, and I blamed the world around me for what I had become.

This phase of rock bottom for me was ironically a very happy and transformative time for my family: my sister had bagged her first role, completed her first film and was on the brink of life-altering fame. The joy I felt for my sister and my pride at her accomplishments was absolute, but her success also threw the disorder in my own life into sharp focus. The insecurities I had as a child—fears that I was lacking—all came rushing back. Everyone in my family belonged to a single industry; my parents, my older siblings, my cousins, my aunts and uncles, and now my younger sister, all made movies. I was surrounded by deeply ambitious, driven, successful, famous people. And here I was—with no more ambition than to leave my bedroom.

I continued to work sporadically throughout my early and mid twenties, and I worked primarily on movies. But consistent, steady work continued to be hard for me. Working during longer depressive episodes took a huge physical and emotional toll because I had to hide and contain the worst of my moods and feelings. During one of the films I worked on as an assistant director, I spent every free second locked in the bathroom or in a secluded corner shaking with tears. I did that for one hundred and twenty days straight.

For the most part when I grew up I felt an internal pressure to follow in the footsteps of my family, even though deep down I knew that it wasn't what came naturally to me. My value system had become muddled and complicated by the success of my family and for a long time, I chased career paths that would lead me to the sort of life I *thought* I should be living. Despite my outgoing personality as a child, I have, as a result of my growing experiences, become a more reserved adult. I'm not a performer or someone who knows how to live in the spotlight. So, I was striving to be someone I no longer was. My reality is different from the reality of my father, mother and sister and it's something I'm still learning to live with. People often ask me if it's difficult to be the only person in my family who isn't famous and my answer to that is: yes, of course it is, but not for the reasons you'd think.

Having been a part of a 'famous family' and having witnessed fame up close my entire life I can tell you that fame isn't 'real'. My sister isn't famous when we're at home dealing with the monotonous details of our day-to-day lives, my mother isn't Soni Razdan, the actor when she's berating me for snapping at her for no good reason, and my father isn't an award-winning director when we're having absurd arguments that only fathers and daughters have. On every single day that does not involve a ridiculously long and tiring award show, or a complicated dash through a crowded airport, my so-called famous family is just beautifully, mundanely human. The issue with fame doesn't come from the value I ascribe to it, rather the value that others ascribe to it. There is a cultural reverence for fame and celebrity that has insidiously convinced us all that we're not enough the way we are, and when the person in the bedroom next to yours is someone who's photographed after a teeth cleaning or when she leaves the gym, there is bound to be an extended amount of confusion. As Chuck Palahniuk's Tyler Durden so poetically put it in *Fight Club*: 'We're the middle children of history. No purpose or place. We have no Great War. No Great Depression. Our Great War's a spiritual war . . . our Great Depression is our lives. We've all been raised on television to believe that one day we'd all be millionaires, and movie gods, and rock stars. But we won't. And we're slowly learning that fact. And we're very, very pissed off.'

Depression deprives you of a good many things on its long, winding course and one of the first things it divests you of is your sense of self. For me, depression's finest feat was tricking me out of an identity and that's not the position you want to find yourself in when you're surrounded by people with such towering, larger-than-life identities of their own. Devoid of an identity I made depression my identity Even when I had finally admitted to being depressed I continued to fight it for a very long time. I didn't know how to separate what I had learned was an illness from my sense of self. I still saw it as a fatal flaw. I began to see my symptoms as defining personality traits rather than what they were: side effects of a troubled mind. When the people in my life told me I was negative, difficult and unfriendly,

I believed that was just who I was deep down inside rather than attributing it to the fact that I was in pain. I embodied my illness and my illness became who I was in my mind.

The realization that depression was *not* my identity came to me as an epiphany, but I can't point to the thought processes that lead to this sudden understanding. I simply woke up one day tired of being boxed in by the labels I had earned over the course of the last twelve years, tired of being restricted by tags of negativity and pessimism. I *wasn't* negative or pessimistic, I realized. If I was an inherently negative person I would never have been able to survive the havoc my mind wreaked. The only reason I made it through so many of my darkest days was that I had hope, a sense of humour and a steadfast belief that my pain didn't signal the end of my life.

I'VE GONE COLD AGAIN.

THE EMOTIONS, THE FEELINGS,

THEY'VE EVAPORATED AGAIN. FOR

A WHILE THERE I FELT DEEPLY.

MORE DEEPLY THAN I HAD IN YEARS. NOW... POOF.

M CONVINCED NC Fake Happy OOMED TO LIVE

Y LIFE TRAPPED IN THIS CYCLE. A CONSTANT RISE

ND FALL PRECIPITATED BY NAIVE HOPE. I FEEL

OLLOW AGAIN. NOTHING SEEMS TO FIT. I DON'T

EEM TO FIT.

Y LIFE..., IT SHOULD BE GOOD.

F I FIND MYSELF COLD NOW,

WILL NEVER BE ABLAZE.

During the sixties and seventies, as a response to preceding and ongoing global violence, the positivity movement was born.

The world had just lived through two World Wars and back home in India, the country was still recovering from the fallout of a bloody and brutal struggle for independence along with the still reverberating after-effects of an equally brutal partition.

This overload of relentless violence gave rise to global non-violence movements, as well as hippie counterculture that preached peace, passivity and a dogged focus on the quest for enlightenment.

One aspect of these counterculture movements—positivity culture—skipped the fence and made the leap from counterculture to mainstream and, today, we're still dealing with the fallout from it. Positivity culture preaches blinkered, single-minded focus on the positive and a commitment to turning a blind eye to anything that is negative.

Positivity culture lives by the old, overused and very misunderstood adage, 'When life hands you lemons, make *lemonade*.' This is a statement we've heard so consistently and for so long that it's now accepted as gospel and we don't even pause to question whether or not it makes sense.[‡]

In our search for silver linings, we've gotten so used to the idea of diverting our attention away from the clouds, that we've lost sight of the sky altogether.

We furiously and constantly avoid or suppress negative feelings and on the off-chance that we do experience them, we make sure to tuck them carefully out of sight so as not to betray any signs of weakness.

We shut down all avenues for vulnerability—shut down any situation that could leave us open to feeling pain or discomfort of any kind. 'Normal and natural emotions are now seen as good or bad and positivity is seen as a new form of moral correctness,' says Susan David, PhD, a psychologist on the faculty of Harvard Medical School and author of the book, *Emotional Agility*. 'People with cancer are automatically told to just stay positive. Women, to stop being so angry.

[‡] https://www.psychologytoday.com/gb/blog/creativity-and-personal-mastery/201004/why-positive-thinking-is-bad-you?page=1

And the list goes on. It's a tyranny. It's a tyranny of positivity. And it's cruel. Unkind. And ineffective. And we do it to others, and we do it to ourselves.'§

Despite all the lessons I've learned over the years, despite all my inward gazing and all the self-awareness I believe I work hard to maintain I have a giant blindspot. I've avoided negative feelings and hidden them away so deftly and for so long, that I didn't even notice that I'm still doing it. I didn't realize I was avoiding negative feelings while *basically making a career of talking about negative feelings.*

I've made an art of talking about my feelings without really acknowledging them or allowing myself to experience them. Even in therapy, I've mastered the skill of talking *around* how I feel with excessive intellectualizations of my emotional states and how I've gotten to be the person I am. I diligently avoid any and all conflict with family members and friends and on the occasions conflict does occur and I find myself overwhelmed, I promptly remove myself from the situation to only cry behind closed doors. If I fail to do so in time, the result is an angry cry-shouting outburst of emotion that only amplifies my anxieties.

---

§ https://www.hopefulminds.co.uk/single-post/2019/07/07/The-Tyranny-of-Relentless-Positivity

I've spent eighteen years feeling my feelings behind closed doors and I've gotten so good at it that I've forgotten how to be vulnerable.

This may not sound like a massive deal.

So I don't like to cry in front of people or talk about what's bothering me. So what? That's okay, right? We all do it.

Except, it really isn't okay. All we're doing when we choose to feel our feeling by ourselves is shut down every possible avenue for vulnerability and as a result, real, meaningful human connections.

We aren't made up of just the happy, jaunty, fair-weather bits of our personalities. The building blocks that make up who we are, are varied. They're of different colours and patterns—I have a leopard-printed one that represents the often questionable taste of the quarter Gujju in me. They come in different sizes—the 'negative body image' block is gargantuan while the 'confidence' block is woefully small. And, different shapes—the 'anxiety' block is both a different shape and size every day.

All these blocks mash together over time like a complicated, never-ending game of Tetris and the end result is us. The more time goes by, the more blocks pile up.

Some of those blocks, or well, if we're being honest—a lot of those blocks—are made up of, or represent things we wish weren't there: Insecurities, grudges, hurt feelings and cleverly built defensive walls.

Research on emotional suppression shows that when emotions are pushed aside or ignored, they only get stronger. Suppressing negative feelings, or insecurities, leads to the worst and most damaging human emotion: shame. The more you hide, the more you feel secretly and in silence, the more that shame grows and flourishes.¶

Shame unravels human connection.** Shame teaches you to hide or pretend because if you show people who you truly are, they will reject you. Shame causes you to isolate yourself from the world around you, shame teaches you to shut down vulnerability because that's how you get hurt. When you allow yourself to be vulnerable you leave yourself open to judgement and ridicule, you give others the chance to see what you think of as the inferior, inept, bad or 'idiot' side of you. The side of you that you've taken great pains to hide away. Yes, vulnerability leaves all those parts of us exposed, but vulnerability also opens us up to some profound rewards.

¶ https://www.hopefulminds.co.uk/single-post/2019/07/07/The-Tyranny-of-Relentless-Positivity
** https://www.cmasas.org/unraveling-shame-and-empathy-dr-brene-brown

Vulnerability is the bedrock upon which real, strong and lasting emotional connections are made. Think about your most important relationships—relationship with your partner, friends, parents or siblings; chances are you've shared more than a few vulnerable moments with them. Vulnerability lets people see you as who you really are and allows you to form relationships based on support and compassion rather than just admiration.

'Vulnerability isn't good or bad,' says Dr Brene Brown. 'It's not what we call a dark emotion, nor is it always a light, positive experience. Vulnerability is the core of all emotions and feelings. To feel is to be vulnerable. To believe vulnerability is a weakness is to believe feeling is a weakness.'

We've spent so long running away from bad feeling that we've forgotten about the genuine value that sadness, pain and strife can add to our lives. We numb bad emotions without realizing that when you try to numb one emotion, you numb them all. Dr Brown goes on to point out that you can't selectively numb the bad without numbing the good. So, when you numb pain, you also effectively numb joy.

'We are caught up in a rigid culture that values relentless positivity over emotional agility, true resilience, and thriving,' says Susan David. 'And when we push aside difficult emotions in order to embrace false positivity, we lose our capacity to develop deep skills to help us deal with the world as it is, not as we wish it to be.'

Depressives resort to silence to cloak shame and avoid vulnerability, almost out of necessity. And every time we choose not to talk about what's really bothering us or disappear behind a locked door to feel our feelings, we hide away a part of who we are, and hiding them away doesn't make those parts disappear. They stay painfully put while we create distance between us and the people we love and who love us.

We wear 'I'm okay' masks, so no one can see how we really feel or ascertain the things that hurt us; we don't show them who we really are, we isolate ourselves when we're in pain and then we spend all our time wondering why no one gets us. They don't get us because they have no idea who we are. How could they? We've never told them.

The advent of technology has also affected the way that positivity culture affects our lives.

We live in strange times.

We live in times of cat GIFs, microwave challenges and videos of perfectly manicured hands kneading slime for 3 minutes that have eight hundred thousand views.

We live in Internet times.

And in these Internet times, we've somehow managed to turn everything, including how we feel, into social currency.

The fallout of the wars that gave birth to the positivity movement was that people became consumed with happiness. It kick-started an almost single-minded obsession with happiness. Hope and positivity became the things to aspire to.

Happiness was fetishized.

For those of us who have come since—there's been little to hurt about.

Yes, we've lived through and witnessed horrific acts of terror but many of us have been lucky and have been kept safely away from the horrors of war.

In times of real war, it took a special sort of brave determination to vow to be peaceful and happy when people were suffering or dying all around—being positive and optimistic in the face of adversity was a mark of strength and bravery because it was hard to be those things.

Today, in the aftermath of that Flower Power culture we somehow believe that our base state is meant to be happiness and any state other than that signals something is wrong.

So in an age where happiness is the norm, being sad and admitting to it is an act of courage and a mark of strength.

Because it's hard to be sad in a happy world.

Just like it was once hard to be happy in a sad world.

Just like we did with happiness, we also fetishized sadness.

Social media is full of examples of the perpetuation of the positivity narrative. Entire lives are being whitewashed and photographed from flattering angles, so much so, that even the so-called highlight reels of our lives are no longer real highlights and are moments that are largely falsified.

But now there's a new narrative slowly creeping up and taking hold—the suffering narrative. Social media is slowly becoming a platform for numerous people, myself included (my first open mention of depression was in an Instagram post), to talk about the various mental health challenges that they face. The Internet seems to suddenly be overrun with talk of depression and anxiety and to a lot of people, I'm sure it seems like half the population has begun to experience these things overnight.

Now, this is obviously not the case—depression and anxiety have been around for as long as we have—and while depression is on the rise, one of the reasons that we are suddenly overrun with accounts of it is because through the efforts of a few pioneer 'over-sharers' and a collective fed up-ness, we have finally begun to see the value in sharing.

I honestly believe that the upsides of this avalanche of sharing we're experiencing outstrip any potential downsides by miles, but, I still think, we need to have a very clear internal awareness and understanding of *why* we share, when we do.

There's a long-standing notion that it's romantic to hurt. The tortured artist is one of the staple figures we've been raised on. 'The brightest flames burn the quickest.' 'Turn your pain into art.' Those are all just ways in which we romanticize pain. We make pain desirable.

Pain and suffering birth creativity.

Pain and suffering birth inevitable triumph.

Pain and suffering birth heroes.

And who doesn't want to be a hero? Mankind has been raised on stories, we are what we are because of the stories we tell, and every story has a protagonist, every story has a hero. And, that's what we are conditioned to chase and aspire to—heroism, through crisis and tragedy and suffering.

Here's the thing though—in all these stories, the heroes don't *think* that they're heroes. They're not doing any of the things that they're doing to be heroes. Whatever they're doing, they're doing to survive.

So many of us unconsciously aspire to the tragedy of being misunderstood because it supposedly leads to heroism or being touted as brave, and I did too, for a time.

As a teenager, I took my angst and spun a romantic tale of untold drama, sadness and misery around it. In this tale, the only way I won, was by not winning. In this tale I succumbed to the darkness within me and the world finally recognized what they hadn't while I was here. That I was meaningful. That I did good. That I was in some way heroic.

How sad that I once believed that my only value was in being tortured and falling victim to that torture.

Talking about how we feel, whether it's in a quiet conversation, a book, a song, an article or a post on social media is one of the most important things we can do for ourselves and those around us right now. But, it's important to know why we're doing it.

Pain has value, yes, but pain and mental illness are not the same thing and mental illnesses can't be seen as a means to an end or a route to greatness. It's not, and it's vital we understand that.

The room is in disarray.

Clothes, shoes and objects at random lay strewn all over the floor and the messy, unmade bed. The table beside it is littered with half-empty tubes of lip-gloss and about six brands of dried out mascara.

Every light in the bedroom has been turned on, its brightness giving the false impression that it's 4 p.m., even though it's closer to nine.

From somewhere on the bed comes the muffled sound of a vibrating phone. It goes unheard thanks to the peppy, upbeat sounds of ABBA blasting through the small speaker in the corner of the room.

At the heart of this disarray is me, my lips a tad too glossy. My hair is being clamped and tugged at by the arms of a straightening iron as I stand in front of the bathroom mirror doing a little jig to 'Voulez Vous'. (Unrelated: I really shouldn't have watched the Mamma Mia musical.)

I rock back and forth, moving and singing along with the music as I force my hair to behave the way I need it to. My fingers accidentally make contact with the straightening iron and I squeal in pain. I turn on the tap and thrust my hand under the cool stream of water. This does nothing to deter the dancing, however, which embarrassingly continues.

The energy in this room is markedly different than it was a month ago. Looking at me now it's impossible to imagine that I could be anything other than the excitable, bubbly entity I currently am. The only remnants of the Feeling's visit——a strip of sedatives and my journal——lie inconspicuously by my bed, unnoticeable to all but me.

In the brief moment of silence leading up to the next ABBA song ('Gimme Gimme Gimme') I hear the phone announce itself and rush out of the bathroom to answer it.

The phone call ends in seconds with a hurried, 'Be down in two minutes.' With a final look in the mirror, I fiddle with my hair and flash myself what I think is a winning smile. It's the first time I'm leaving the house, ready to engage with the outside world, in weeks, and I've all but forgotten that fact.

The Feeling has left, for the time being, and now that it has, it's almost impossible to remember what it truly felt like while it was here. My mind has chosen selective amnesia and wiped the worst of it from memory so I'm left to contend with only a hazy fear of the Feeling's return.

In fact, I almost believe I've seen the last of it. Almost. I've been here a hundred times before, relaxed and forgetful, but I know now from all those previous times that it won't last. As surely as I'm happy now, I will be sad tomorrow. As surely as the Feeling has left, it will return. But that's okay, because my life is no longer about running away from depression. It is about walking alongside it.

I grab my bag and waft out of the bedroom door, leaving it wide open behind me. Above it, the clock, restored to its home on the inside wall, steadily ticks time away.

EN TO PAPER.

ATHER. RINSE. REPEAT.

Y CONTINUED BEING WEARS ME DOWN. THE EARTH

URNS, DAYS, TIME, GOES BY — NOTHING SHIFTS.

HE HOLLOW STAYS WHERE IT FIRMLY TOOK ROOT ALL

HOSE YEARS AGO.

Y MIND, MY BODY, Let It Be T LEARN. THEY DON'T

HANGE. THEY DON'T STOP.

ELF-DESTRUCTION IS THE ONLY WAY FORWARD.

HY ELSE HAVE I BEEN ON A CRASH COURSE SINCE

ACHIEVED COGINISANCE.

Y ELSE HAVE I CYCLED BETWEEN DESPERATE

TEMPTS TO CLING ONTO THE HUMAN EXPERIENCE

D DETERMINED ATTEMPTS TO ABANDON IT

NTIRELY.

ER SINCE I CAN REMEMBER I HAVE FURIOUSLY

ASED THE THRILL AND ACHE AND PAIN OF

TACHMENT. AND EVERY SINGLE TIME I HAVE FOUND

YSLEF, BY MISTAKE OR DESIGN, BACK HERE.

FEELING BLANKNESS. DETACHMENT.

RD IN THE FACE OF EVERYTHING SOFT.

E IN THE FACE OF BLAZING FIRE.

T BROKEN. YET TIRED. YET LONELY. YET STUBBORNLY.

UMAN.

OICE. FREE WILL. JOY. WORDS THAT DON'T LEAD TO ONE

NOTHER.

T AGAIN ON THE VERGE OF CAUSING IMMEASURABLE

AIN. YET AGAIN ON THE BRINK OF LOSS.

The way I've told it, it may seem like I'm suggesting my whole adult life has been nothing but a steady stream of misery with absolutely no bright spots. On the contrary, my life so far has been a roller coaster of highs and lows, full of the joys of true love, happiness, friendship and companionship. But this is what depression does; it robs you even of joyous hindsight. It poisons your mind and obscures all the good in your life. All the positive, alive moments of life seem like distant, long-lost memories and all that you can see in the rear-view mirror is the pain you've left behind.

'What's wrong with me?' I remember despondently asking my father one evening, many years ago. We had lapsed into a comfortable silence during an unrelated discussion when the question came bursting out of me.

'Why don't I know how to be happy?'

My father surveyed me intently for a moment.

'And why do you want to be happy?' he asked.

It seemed like an absurd question.

'What do you mean "why"?' I shot back. 'Everyone wants to be happy.'

'Why?' he pressed.

'I don't know . . . who wants to be sad all the time? It's not normal, and it's exhausting.'

He smiled slightly.

'You want to be happy because society has convinced you that so-called "normal" people are happy all the time. You want to be happy because you want to fit in,' he said simply.

'And why should you fit into the parameters of some made-up definition of normalcy?' he continued, as my brow furrowed in thought. 'You're exhausted because you're always pretending to be something you're not. You're constantly trying to reach this non-existent, ideal state of emotional well-being. It's not real. You're being set up to fail.'

'So then what do I do?' I asked miserably.

'Take off the mask. You aren't happy? Fine, you aren't happy. One day you will be. And then you'll be sad again. Accept that and stop wasting your energy chasing something that doesn't exist. You can't spend your life feeling bad about feeling bad.'

That sleepless night I pondered over my father's words. He was right. The more I tried and failed at being content the worse I felt because I was failing at yet another thing.

This realization for me was the beginning of genuine acceptance, and the more I thought about it, the more I realized that most of our problems in life stem from the quest for permanence. In this age of instant gratification we want everything in our lives to come without an expiry date. We want everything to be permanent— relationships, love, beauty, youth, *happiness.* But the truth is, permanence is an illusion, and like everything else in life, happiness also comes and goes. Trying to be happy forever is like trying to stop water from slipping through your fingers. It's not possible, and the only way forward is to realize and accept it.

The only permanent fixture in life is change. Change. Change. Change.

And oddly enough, it's this one truth of life that causes me so much distress and it is also the very thing that helps me feel better. On the one hand, it's the awareness of constant change and transience that sends me into a spiral of anxiety, while on the other, it's hugely freeing to realize that nothing I have now, not even my emotional state of mind, is going to stay the same.

I chose to accept pain, even though I hated it. Pain, up to a certain degree, is good. Discomfort is not a bad thing, and it's one of the few emotional states that encourages growth. Physical exercise involves discomfort, but it's an example of a good sort of pain. Pain that helps you grow. Mental and psychological aches, when they're not severe, are good for you in a similar way. It doesn't feel great while it's happening but you are better for having lived through it.

Happiness is a beautiful, enjoyable feeling to have, and we should, by all means, enjoy it while it lasts. But to me, it's always been the least transformative of the emotions. Happiness is a one-note emotion that doesn't challenge you in any way. I've learned so much about myself and who I am over the last sixteen years only because of the discomfort I've endured. The state of mind I was in, forced me to question everything and that's where learning begins—with questions. It is in sadness that I have travelled to the depths of my soul and been acquainted with its weather-worn exterior. And it is in sorrow that I have learned to tap into the abundant life force held safely within.

For a lot of people acceptance signals failure or resignation, but in my understanding it's quite the opposite. The only way to solve a problem is to accept that it exists in its current form. And, solving a problem doesn't always mean eliminating it entirely. For many people like myself, depression is an ongoing affliction, and it isn't something that can be completely stamped out. Acceptance also means I had to readjust my value system based on the limitations that depression caused. For me depression is debilitating and when it's present, I'm unable to function. I had to come to terms with the fact that my mind was different and as a result of that so was my life. I couldn't push pause on everything and hold out for complete recovery because if I did, I would be waiting a very long time.

I am who I am in the now, and I have to work my life around that. That isn't giving up; it's adjusting to the reality of my condition and giving myself a higher chance of living a successful life by not chasing after unrealistic goals.

This sense of acceptance also eventually led me to something wonderful and transforming: gratitude; a profound sense of gratitude for what depression has given me, rather than what it has taken away.

They say that in order to experience true happiness you have to have first felt pain. I am certainly no stranger to pain. I've experienced a great deal of it, as have so many of us. But the wonderful upside to experiencing all that pain is the deep appreciation I have for moments in which my life and mind are devoid of pain, and moments that even (shockingly) contain joy. The big-picture vantage point I believe I have, the one that has always underlined and highlighted the futility of life and the imminence of death, has also quietly done something else to me. Over the years it has discreetly, without my knowledge, introduced me to the things that truly matter. It has made me aware of how little the many things we place so much value on actually matter. One of the strangest things about living with chronic depression is living with the knowledge that it's always in my future. No matter how good or peaceful I feel right now, it's always lurking around the corner. Walking around with the fear of when my depression will return is terrifying, but it's also extremely humbling as it serves as a potent reminder of the truly meaningful things in my life. It has, bizarrely, made me a calmer person.

Depression has given me perspective. My notions of success, beauty, fame, power—ideas that controlled me for so long—have all changed. I'm not entirely immune to them—I'm only human—and there are many days on which feelings of inferiority take hold of me. But on days like that I just need reminding. It has magnified and multiplied the empathy within me and it has fanned the sparks of creativity. It has taught me how to be alone and how to find comfort in myself. It has made me love more fiercely and with abandon. It has not simply made me tolerant of the differences of others, it has shone a light on the beauty of that dissimilarity. It showed me that just because you don't understand something it doesn't mean it's bad or wrong or that it needs to be feared. It showed me that most of the anger and negativity around us stems from fear, and it showed me kindness is the only way forward.

My story is not the story of someone who walked through the fires of hell to come out on the other side unharmed and unscathed. My story is not the story of someone who survived to then disappear into the mountains and live out the rest of her life in peace and tranquility as someone fixed and healed. That's the unrealistic version of life we all want to live. The one where we freeze frame at the end of the movie and the words 'and she lived happily ever after' appear on the screen in pretty loopy handwriting.

That's a fairy tale.

And I refuse to be co-opted by a fairy tale.

Perpetual bliss does not exist and anyone who peddles the belief that it does, or tries to convince you that there is a secret path through the woods that leads to an oasis of unending peace and happiness is either deluded, or a liar.

For too long we've been convinced that the emotional fairy tale—the perfect state of emotional well-being— exists, and that it's tantalizingly close but just out of reach. We've been convinced that it exists and we've been convinced that there's something fundamentally wrong with us for not being able to attain it.

It's high time that we realize that there's nothing wrong with us.

There's something wrong with the fairy tale. Perpetual bliss does not exist, and saying that does not make me a nihilist.

I sit on the same see-saw that we all do and it continuously goes up and down, shifting between darkness and light—it's the same for us all. Some of us simply stay down a little longer in a dark that's just a little darker.

Transience is something we're all so afraid of, and we live in perpetual fear of a new, different reality.

But thank God for transience because even though it means that happiness doesn't last it also means that pain eventually passes.

It means that neither heaven nor hell are permanent.

There is nothing glorious or freeing or romantic or lovely about depression. Depression is a monster, a villain and thief, but even the worst of experiences teach you something. Depression has taken a lot from me and it has also given me a lot, but only because I eventually demanded it. I demanded my lessons and I took them head on.

'You must not allow your pain to be wasted, Shaheen,' my father said to me. I chant that quietly to myself—'My pain must not be wasted,' I say—and I try to *learn*, I try to *do*. I grieve and cry and hurt but I also take my medication and go to therapy. I watch my soul being bent and twisted into painful, unnatural shapes and marvel at how I've never seen it from those angles before. There are still days and weeks and months when I am also consumed by depression, when I forget all my lessons, when I forget everything but the pain. And that's also when I turn to the very idea I'm afraid of: transience.

I remind myself if happiness is fleeting, then so is sadness.

I remind myself depression is the weather, and I'm a weather-worn tree.

I remind myself even the worst storms pass.

I remind myself I've survived them all.

26.11.2016

...AY NOW HAVE AS MANY NOTEBOOKS AS THOUGHTS.
...UPPOSE THERE ARE WORSE PROBLEMS TO HAVE. I
...METIMES THINK I HAVE WORSE PROBLEMS. I
...L AS THOUGH - SUDDENLY - THOSE PROBLEMS ARE
...MATERIAL. I Acknowledgements N'T WRITE
...OUT THEM.

* * * * *

...TEMPT # 2

...ERE IS A FEELING THAT MY WORDS WILL
...IVIALISE ALL THAT I FEEL. THAT ONCE I SAY IT, IT'S
...RIVIAL. BECAUSE WHY SHOULDN'T IT BE.
...L THAT HAS GONE ON IN THE WORLD - ALL
...AT IS GOING ON - WHY SHOULD HOW I FEEL BE
...NYTHING.
...HOW I FEEL IS THE BY-PRODUCT OF AN
...VOLVED BRAIN. MY FEELINGS ARE EVOLUTIONARY
...OLLATERAL DAMAGE.

...FEEL LIKE I DON'T BELONG HERE.
...ECAUSE IF I DID, I WOULD KNOW HOW TO BE
...ERE. I WOULD NOT FEEL SO TRAPPED IN MY
...ODY - IN MY LIFE. IN MY DEATH.
...AM NOT SUPPOSED TO DIE BECAUSE I WAS NEVER
...PPOSED TO BE ALIVE.
...M CONFINED TO MY BODY. CONFINED TO MY MIND. I'M A
...ELING. NOT A PERSON.
...M UNABLE TO PROCESS ALL THE PAIN AROUND ME.

I would like to thank:

Papa, everything I know of being human, I've learned from you.

Rukun and Naomi, for giving me the ultimate shot at catharsis—with one little meeting at a Bandra tea room you offered me the chance to redefine my relationship with myself.

Gurveen, for your enduring patience and gentle prodding. Thank you for lending your voice to my story and pushing me to dig even deeper when all I wanted to do was take a big, long nap.

Acknowledgements

Dipti, my guiding light on this very daunting and transformative journey—baring my soul to you could not have been easier or more rewarding.

Dorita, meticulous and ever-watchful—thank you for having my back and putting up with my consistently appalling response times to absolutely everything.

My family, my beating heart.

My grandparents Nindi and Trudy—all that I am begins with you. Thank you for my childhood and everything that has come since.

My friends. Old, new, past and present. You know who you are. You've held me together.

Every single person who has ever written me a kind message, letter or comment. This book was borne from the knowledge that I am not alone. Thank you for showing me every day that we're all in this together.

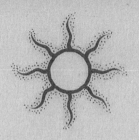

'TH JUNE 2007

HATE MY LIFE. MY SI... References ...HATE EVERYTHING
BOUT THIS LITTLE UNIVERSE OF MINE.
LL I HAVE EVER MANAGED TO DO IS FEEL STUPID
ND TALENTLESS. I FELT STUPID IN SCHOOL WHERE I
AILED EVERYTHING EVERY YEAR. I FEEL STUPID IN
OLLEGE WHERE-SAME THING. I FEEL STUPID AROUND
RIENDS AND IN RELATIONSHIPS.
ND I FEEL, STUPID, NO-GOOD, DIFFICULT AND LIKE A
FAILURE AT HOME.
F SOMEONE'S BEEN PLANNING THIS, THEY'VE WON.
FEEL NO GOOD. LIKE LIKE A DUCK AMONG SWANS.
AND SOMEWHERE I HATE THE WORLD FOR DOING
THIS TO ME. SETTING ME UP TO THESE STANDARDS
CAN'T MEET. MAKING IT ALL MY FAULT.
WANT TO IMPLODE, TO DISAPPEAR.
NYTHING TO STOP GRAPPLING WITH MY OWN
MEDIOCRITY. I'M A FAILURE AT EVERYTHING. BE IT
SCHOOL, COLLEGE, FRIENDSHIPS OR RELATIONSHIPS.
HE UNIVERSE SHOULD JUST WEED ME OUT RIGHT NOW. IT'S
URVIVAL OF THE FITTEST THING WILL NOT WORK
KE THIS.

W hile every effort has been made to ensure the accuracy and completeness of this list I apologize for any errors or omissions and would be grateful if I am notified of any corrections that should be incorporated in future reprints or editions of this book.

1. 'Causes of Depression'. WebMD. https://www.webmd.com/depression/guide/causes-depression#1.
2. 'Depression'. The National Institute of Mental Health, February 2018. https://www.nimh.nih.gov/health/topics/depression/index.shtml.
3. 'Depression—Let's Talk'. World Health Organization, 7 April 2017. http://www.who.int/mental_health/management/depression/en/.
4. Foer, Jonathan Safran. *Extremely Loud and Incredibly Close*. Wilmington: Mariner Books, 2005.

5. Jamison, Kay Redfield. *An Unquiet Mind: A Memoir of Moods and Madness.* New York: A.A. Knopf, 1995.

6. Kerr, Michael. 'Major Depressive Disorder (Clinical Depression)'. *Healthline,* 2017. https://www. healthline.com/health/clinical-depression#causes.

7. MacGill, Markus. 'What Is Depression and What Can I Do About It?' *Medical News Today,* 30 November 2017. https://www.medicalnewstoday.com/kc/ depression-causes-symptoms-treatments-8933.

8. Merkin, Daphne. *This Close to Happy: A Reckoning with Depression.* New York: Farrar, Straus and Giroux, 2017.

9. Miranda, Lin-Manuel. 'Hamilton: An American Musical'. *Hamilton: The Revolution.* Edited by Jeremy McCarter. New York: Grand Central Publishing, 2016.

10. Palahniuk, Chuck. *Fight Club.* New York: W.W. Norton & Company, 1996.

11. Plath, Sylvia. *The Unabridged Journals of Sylvia Plath.* New York: Anchor, 1982.

12. Schimelpfening, Nancy. 'The 9 Most Common Causes of Depression'. *Very Well Mind,* 30 April 2018.

13. Solomon, Andrew. *The Noonday Demon: An Anatomy of Depression.* New York: Scribner, 2002.

14. Tatera, Kelly. 'Shame is Actually Critical for Our Survival, Researchers Argue.' http://

thescienceexplorer.com/brain-and-body/shame-actually-critical-our-survival-researchers-argue

15. Wallace, David Foster. *Infinite Jest.* New York: Bay Back Books, 1996.
16. 'What Is Depression?' American Psychiatric Association, January 2017. https://www.psychiatry.org/patients-families/depression/what-is-depression.

Further Reading

Some books I have found to be brilliant, insightful and helpful:

The Noonday Demon: An Atlas of Depression—Andrew Solomon

First, We Make the Beast Beautiful—Sarah Wilson

Furiously Happy: A Funny Book about Horrible Things—Jenny Lawson

An Unquiet Mind: A Memoir of Moods and Madness—Kay Redfield Jamison

Reasons to Stay Alive—Matt Haig

This Close to Happy—Daphne Merkin

Staring at the Sun—Irvin Yalom

Darkness Visible—William Styron

Feeling Good the New Mood Therapy—David Burns

A Note on the Author

Shaheen Bhatt is a screenwriter and has lived with depression for close to twenty years. She recently launched Here Comes the Sun—a mental health awareness initiative and support system for people living with mental illness. She was born in Bombay and lives there with her attention-seeking family and her three cats—Sheba, Pica and Edward.

Notes

_____
_____
_____
_____
_____
_____
_____
_____
_____
_____
_____
_____
_____
_____

)❶○❶(

☽◗●◗☾

☽◑◯◐☾

꒰ ꒱ ◯ ꒰ ꒱

))●○●((

꒰ ꒱꒰꒰꒱꒱꒰ ꒱